Workpapers Concerning
Waorani Discourse Features

Summer Institute of Linguistics
**Language Data
Amerindian Series**

Publication Number 10

Viola Waterhouse
Series Editor

William R. Merrifield
*Editor-in-chief
Academic Publications Coordinator*

Workpapers Concerning Waorani Discourse Features

Evelyn G. Pike

and

Rachel Saint

Editors

A Publication of
The Summer Institute of Linguistics, Inc.

Dallas

LANGUAGE DATA is a serial publication of the Summer Institute of Linguistics, Inc. The series is intended as an outlet for data-oriented papers authored by members of the Institute. All volumes are issued as microfiche editions, while certain selected volumes are also printed in off-set editions. A listing of available volumes will be sent upon request.

Copyright ©1988 by the Summer Institute of Linguistics, Inc.
Library of Congress Catalog No: 88-62278
ISBN: 0-88312-625-7
ISSN: 1040-1113

Printed in the United States of America
All Rights Reserved

No part of this publication may be reproduced, stored in a retrieval system, or transmitted in any form or by any means—electronic, mechanical, photocopy, recording, or otherwise—without the express permission of the Summer Institute of Linguistics, with the exception of brief excerpts in journal articles or reviews.

Copies of this and other publications of the Summer Institute of Linguistics may be obtained from

Academic Book Center
Summer Institute of Linguistics
7500 W. Camp Wisdom Rd.
Dallas, TX 75236

Contents

Preface ix
Abbreviations and Symbols xiii
References xvii

PART I
Some Grammatical Structures of Discourse

Michael Miller: What Can Mark the Peak of a Story? 3
Deborah Ross: Chronological and Logical Discourse Chains 9
Carol Hepner: Hypothesis on Helping to Identify Waorani Discourse Types 15
Mary E. Holman: The Function of ayæ 'then' in Waorani 17
Mark Hepner: Thematic Unity as Evidence for the Presence of Paragraphs 23

PART II
Some Grammatical Structures from Discourse to Morpheme Classes

Evelyn G. Pike: Trees for Constituent Analysis, from Discourse to Morpheme 31
Patricia Wilkendorf: Waorani Clauses 47
Thomas W. Holman: Waorani Verb Affixes 57

PART III
Some Referential Structures of Discourse

Patricia Wilkendorf: Notes on Referential Elements in Three Texts . 75
Leoma Gilley: How to Know What to Remember—Affixal Clues ... 89
Lynn Zander: Keeping Track of Participants Where They Are Not Named 93
Timothy Wilt: Prominence of Waves of Space and Time 99

PART IV
The Texts

The Origin of the Rainbow by Dayuma 105
The Jaguar and the Turtle by Giketa 107
The Origin of the Corn Bees by Dayuma 115
The Origin of Cassava by Dayuma 119
The Spider Monkey's Tail by Giketa 125
The Spider Monkey's Thumbs by Giketa 129
The Tapir by Giketa 133
The Alligator and the Bird by Giketa 145
Bluebird's Report by Wiña 151
Waorani Earholes by Akawo 161

Preface

For approximately two decades one of the editors, Rachel Saint, lived in eastern Ecuador among a group calling themselves Waorani, who have been popularly known as Aucas (a term derived from Quichua meaning 'savage'). Early in that period she learned the language and collected, with their help, various taped legends and descriptions of events. Here we wish to make available to persons interested in that language and culture a literal and free translation of some of these materials.

But it seemed possible, with the help of the other editor, to do more than that. Evelyn Pike, with Timothy Wilt as an assistant, was teaching, at the University of Texas at Arlington, a group of students who were in general, in the second semester of their linguistic program. Pike thought it would be an exciting assignment for them to try to apply to these texts some of the tagmemic principles represented in the textbook of which she was coauthor (Pike and Pike 1982, 2nd edition. This reference as well as several others have been updated since the workpapers were completed in 1980) as well as the principles emphasized in the suggested readings of other scholars on discourse—especially those of Longacre (1967, 1976a, 1976b, 1979), Grimes (1975, 1978), Linda K. Jones (1977), and Larson (1978). This resulted in term papers, from some of which the accompanying excerpts have been taken.

Some important and helpful prior work on Waorani was available to them for grammatical analysis. This included, principally, the technical grammar by Peeke (1973) as well as her pedagogical grammar (1979). It seemed desirable, however, to try—in the present climate of research—to go beyond these, into the area of discourse. In her earlier work, Peeke (1973:11,13) had said that "Assertion of primacy of the sentence in grammar does not necessarily preclude recognition of syntactic structure in such more-inclusive types as the paragraph, although syntactic paragraph structure is not apparent in [Waorani]. Examples so far cited of structure in this more diffuse area have the earmarks of semantic rather than of syntactic structure, in my opinion.... Since this present syntactic model exists to generate sentences, no attempt is made to describe discourse structure per se, but only that information about discourse which may be directly mapped onto individual sentences is discussed." The papers given here struggle to enter a bit further into this little-known territory, seeking to find both grammatical structures and referential ones above the sentence. Because the students used only a few of the shorter texts, their hypotheses would be subject to revision if they were to consider more data.

In Part I the papers select specific items which characterize the grammar of discourse as a whole—or that of paragraph or subsection. (These papers often take their theoretical stimulous from Longacre and Grimes.) Miller, for example, discusses how to recognize the peak of a story. Ross discusses chaining—linking of a particular kind—in a story. Carol Hepner treats tense as related to discourse. Mary Holman follows one particle in its function throughout a text. Mark Hepner finds oral paragraphs.

In Part II the Pike and Pike model for grammar is basic to the presentations. Evelyn Pike first gives a preliminary grammatical tree sketch for a text as a whole from discourse to morpheme, with slot and role noted on the branches of the tree and class given at the end of the branches. This emphasizes a continuity of the theory and technology which allows no major break from the whole text to the smallest constituent. She then treats a second text in less detail. Transition from etic tree structures to emic formulas (from the particular, guessed-at structure to a more formal checked-out generalization of various such subtrees) is provided at the clause level by Wilkendorf, and at the verb level by Thomas Holman. In these latter two papers, the tagmeme is especially seen as a unit-in-context, with the four cell requirement of Pike and Pike for adequate representation: slot for insistence on an including context, role for function in relation to other immediate constituents of the including context, class for the substance of the manifesting form, cohesion for the controlling and controlled elements of agreement and government.

Part III has two different styles of analysis included. It begins with the Pike and Pike type of treatment of the referential hierarchy (the structure of happening, rather than the grammatical, linear structure of its telling—the structure of what the speech refers to). Wilkendorf treats three texts from this viewpoint in a preliminary attempt to carry further the suggestions for the analysis outlined in the classroom. Then (reminiscent again of Longacre and Grimes) in a treatment of more focussed specific problems, Gilley discusses the relation of some affixes to the referential hierarchy. Zander discusses ways of keeping track of the identity of participants at points in a story where they are not named. And Wilt suggests a hypothesis to the effect that time and space might be treated in the slot cell, from a wave perspective.

Part IV gives text material with literal and free translations. This includes stories which, because they were short, served, largely, for the student analyses mentioned above. These had appeared previously in the

Waorani language, without analyses or translation, in reading readiness primers for the Waorani people (Saint 1967, 1968). Some further texts, with content of various kinds, and of possible anthropological interest, are also given. Sentences in the papers having numbers higher than those given in the texts refer to supplementary data given to the students, but not included here. They were of a type which an analyst of the language would have collected before beginning serious analysis of the language texts.

·We would like to express our thanks to the Waorani narrators who provided Rachel Saint with the material, and to the Ecuadorian government for giving us access to the fascinating part of the country where this language is spoken. We are also grateful to Kenneth L. Pike for reading the manuscripts in draft, making suggestions about some of the materials in them most likely to be of interest to our readers, and suggesting, also, ways to help the reader sense more easily the coherence of these different items within an overall approach to the theory and study of discourse.

Evelyn G. Pike and Rachel Saint
Norman, Oklahoma
July 27, 1980

Abbreviations of Terms and Symbols

A	actor	Inton	intonation
Admon	admonstrative	It	item
Adv	adverb	Limit	limiter
Asser	assertive	Loc	location
Aux	auxiliary	M	mode
BI	biintransitive	Man	manner
BT	bitransitive	Mar	margin
Cert	certainty	N	noun
Circum	circumstance	Neg	negative
Cl	clause	Nuc	nucleus
Clstr	cluster	OK	all right
Cmnt	comment	P	predicate/phrase
Cnst	contrast	Per	person
Com	command	Perf	perfect
Conseq	consequence	Perm	permanent
Cs	cause	Permis	permission
Dep	dependent	Perm.st	permanent state
Deris	derisive	Pred	predication
Dubi	dubious	Pn	pronoun
Ef	effect	Prop	proposition
Emph	emphasis	Pst	past
Exclam	exclamatory	Pt of Ref	point of reference
Excl	exclusive	Refl	reflexive
Expan	expansion	Remonst	remonstrate
Expl	expletive	Rt	root
Fut	future	Sc	scope
H	honorific	Seq	sequence
HC	hyperclass	Sent	sentence
I	intransitive	Sp	speech
Id	identifier	Sta	statement
Imp	imperative	Suf	suffix
Incep	inception	T	transitive
Incl	inclusive	Tm	time
Ind	independent	Ts	tense
Infer	inference	Twd	toward
Instr	instruction	U	undergoer
Intens	intensifier	V	verb

1, 2, 3	first, second, third person singular
1d, 2d, 3d	first, second, third person dual
1p, 2p, 3p	first, second, third person plural
¶	paragraph
?	interrogative intonation
x (y)	morpheme variants

Abbreviations of the Titles of the Texts

AB	The Alligator and the Bird
BR	Bluebird's Report
CB	The Origin of the Corn Bees
EH	Waorani Earholes
JT	The Jaguar and the Turtle
OC	The Origin of Cassava
OR	The Origin of the Rainbow
TH	The Spider Monkey's Thumbs
TL	The Spider Monkey's Tail
TP	The Tapir

Some Idioms and Names from the Texts

awǽpayegõ: awǽpaye-gõ	thumb-finger.id 'thumb'
ayǽ: a-yǽ	see-much 'then'
æbã̄nõ: æ-bã(ã̄)-nõ	interr-whole-twd another 'how'
ædõmẽ: æ-dõ-mẽ	interr-twd.another 'speculate'
ædõnõ: æ-dõ-nõ	interr-twd.another-trail.id 'where'
ænõmẽ-nãni	lowland-3p 'lowlanders' (generally known as the downriver group)
badõ-ŋã: ba-dõ-ŋã	become-twd.another-3 'create-3'
bedõ: be-dõ	drink-twd.another 'drown'
botõmokã: bo-tõ-mo-kã	1-pn-seed-3 'my grandchild'
daimẽ: dai-mẽ	clay-vine 'rainbow'
ẽã: ẽ-ã	exist-say 'exist'
ga-bi	roll-2 'plant (by rolling stalk into the ground)'
gĩĩ (be-kã-ĩ)	little drink-3-be 'become thin'
godõ: go-dõ	go-twd another 'trail' (dõ 'trail id')
iña-nãni	fellow-2p 'you fellows, you dear ones'
ĩnõ: ĩ-nõ	be-twd.another 'there'
ĩñõmõ: ĩ-ñõ-mõ	be-where-perm.st 'there'
ĩñõtobǽ: ĩ-ñõ-to-bǽ	be-where-cut-divide 'suddenly'
kadæ:	(Dayuma's grandfather's name)
kapitãã	pilot 'captain' (recent Spanish loan)
kǽmǽ:	(name of Giketa's daughter)
kǽyǽ: kǽyǽ	cook-much 'cookpot'
kẽwe: kẽ-wẽ	live-always.id 'cassava' (staff of life)
kĩnõ: kĩ-nõ	interr-twd.another 'what'
kĩn(õ)ãte: kĩ-n(õ)-ã-te	interr-twd.another-say-ing 'why'
kõwẽ: kõ-wẽ	?-always.id 'always'
mãniñõmõ: mãni-ño-mõ	this-where-perm.st 'right here'

mãnĩñõmõ:	mãnĩ-ñõ-mõ	over.there-where-perm.st 'over there'
mĩkaye:		'wasp', name of Dayuma's brother
nõwoõnæ:	ñõwo-õnæ	now-day 'today'
ñæ̃wæ̃næ̃:		name of the jaguar
ñõwõõnæ:	ñõwo-õnæ	now-day 'today'
odæ:	ãa-dẽ	pick bathe-perf 'preen feathers'
õnõ:	õ-nõ	?-twd.another 'river'
õnõkado:	õnõ-kado	body-nose.id 'nose'
õnõmõka:	õnõ-mõka	body-ear.id 'ear'
õñõ-pa:	õ-ñõ-pa	?-lie-asser 'lies'
	õõ-kæ-te	blow-incep-ing 'hunting (with a blow gun)'
	õntoka-do	stick-out.of 'limb'
põnẽ:	põ-nẽ	come-perf 'remember, believe'
põnõ-mĩni:	põ-nõ-mĩni	come-twd.another-2p 'you (pl) give'
tæiyæ̃:	tæi-yæ̃	many-much 'lots'
tõmãã:	tõ-mãã	pn-all 'all'
wadæ:	wa-dæ	other.id-none 'away'
wãtapiyæ̃-:	wãta-pi-yæ̃	little.while-long-much 'long time'
wepæ̃:	we-pæ̃	red-liquid.id 'blood'
	yæ-dẽ-mæ̃-mõ	expand-inside-arm.id-perm.st 'stalk'
yædẽmadã:	yæ-dẽ-madã	extend-perf-mother 'pregnant'
yægĩkamẽ:	yægĩka-mẽ	certain.bush-vine.id
yæwa:	yæ-wa	expand-foot.id 'root'
yiko:		a girl's name

References

Beekman, John and John Callow. 1979. The semantic structure of written communication. Fourth revision. Dallas: Summer Institute of Linguistics.

Derbyshire, Desmond C. 1979. Discourse redundancy in Hixkaryana. In Beekman and Callow 1979. Dallas: Summer Institute of Linguistics.

Frank, David Benjamin. 1977. Some principles of higher level linguistic analysis as applied to 'The fable of the good lions.' Unpublished M.A. thesis. University of Texas at Arlington.

Gibbs, William P. 1977. Discourse elements in Sierra de Juárez Zapotec. Unpublished M.A. thesis. The University of Texas at Arlington.

Grimes, Joseph E. 1967. Positional analysis. Language 43:437–44.

———. 1975. The thread of discourse. The Hague. Mouton.

———. 1978. A heuristic for paradigms. In David L. Waltz (ed), Theoretical issues and natural processing 2:232–35. Urbana: University of Illinois Press.

———, Ivan Lowe, and Robert A. Dooley. 1978. Closed systems with complex restrictions. Anthropological Linguistics 20:167–83.

Halliday, M.A.K. and Ruqaiya Hasan. 1976. Cohesion in English. London: Longman.

Howland, Lillian G. 1981. Communicational integration of reality and fiction. Language and Communication 1.89–148.

Hwang, Shin Ja. 1979. The referential hierarchical structure of a Korean folktale. Unpublished ms.

Jenner, Phillip N. (ed). 1978. Mon Khmer Studies 7. Honolulu: University of Hawaii.

Jones, Larry B. and Linda K. Jones. 1979a. Multiple levels of information in discourse. In Linda K. Jones (ed), Discourse studies in

Mesoamerican Languages, 1:3–29. Summer Institute of Linguistics and the University of Texas at Arlington Publications in Linguistics 58.

Jones, Larry B. and Donald Nellis. 1979b. A discourse particle in Cajonos Zapotec. In Linda K. Jones (ed), Discourse studies in Mesoamerican languages, 1:189–218. Summer Institute of Linguistics and the University of Texas at Arlington Publications in Linguistics 55.

Jones, Linda K. 1977. Theme in English expository discourse. Lake Bluff: Jupiter Press.

Koontz, Carol and Joanne Anderson. 1977. Connectives in Teribe. In Robert E. Longacre (ed), Discourse grammar: studies in indigenous languages of Columbia, Panama, and Ecuador, 2:95–131. Summer Institute of Linguistics Publications in Linguistics and Related Fields 52.

Larson, Mildred Lucille. 1978. The functions of reported speech in discourse. Summer Institute of Linguistics and the University of Texas at Arlington Publications in Linguistics 59.

Longacre, Robert E. 1968. Comparative reconstruction of indigenous languages. The Hague. Mouton.

———. 1976a. Review of some aspects of text grammars by T. A. van Dijk. Journal of Linguistics 12.169–74.

———. 1976b. An anatomy of speech notions. Lisse: The Peter de Ridder Press.

———. 1977. A discourse manifesto. Notes on Linguistics 4:17–29. Dallas: Summer Institute of Linguistics.

———. 1979. The paragraph as a grammatical unit. In Talmy Givon (ed), Discourse and Syntax. New York: Academic Press.

——— and Stephen H. Levinsohn. 1978. Field analysis of discourse. In Wolfgang Dressler (ed), Current trends in text linguistics 103–22. Berlin: Walter de Gruyter.

Marchese, Lynn. 1978. Time reference in Godié. In Joseph E. Grimes (ed), Papers on discourse, 63–75. Summer Institute of Linguistics Publications in Linguistics and Related Fields 51.

Peeke, M. Catherine. 1973. Preliminary Grammar of Auca. Summer Institute of Linguistics Publications in Linguistics and Related Fields 39.

———. 1979. El idioma huao: gramática pedagógica, tomo 1. Cuadernos etnolingüísticos 3. Quito: Instituto Lingüístico de Verano.

Pike, Kenneth L. 1964. Stress trains in Auca. In David Abercrombie and others (eds), In Honour of Daniel Jones: papers contributed on the occasion of his eightieth birthday, September 12, 1961. Pp. 425–31. London: Longmans.

—— and Evelyn G. Pike. [1977] 1982. Grammatical analysis. 2nd ed. Dallas: Summer Institute of Linguistics and the University of Texas at Arlington Publications in Linguistics 53.

—— and ——. 1983. Text and tagmeme. Norwood: Ablex.

Powlison, Paul S. 1965. A paragraph analysis of a Yagua folktale. International Journal of American Linguistics 31:109–18.

Saint, Rachel. 1964a. Leyenda de como nacen los niños aucas; Auca Childbirth Legend, según la versión del tío Giquita (Spanish and English versions). Quito: Instituto Lingüístico de Verano.

——. 1964b. Leyenda de los aucas y los caníbales, según la versión del tío Giquita (Spanish and English versions). Quito: Instituto Lingüístico de Verano.

——. 1967. Titæque tonõ Meñe. Giqueta apænekã, Waorani. Quito: Instituto Lingüístico de Verano.

——. 1968a. Dayomæ apænekã. Waorani. Quito: Instituto Lingüístico de Verano.

——. 1968b. Biwii tonõ Nom̃a. Giqueta apænekã, Waorani. Quito: Instituto Lingüístico de Verano.

——. 1968c. Deye. Giqueta apænekã, Waorani. Quito: Instituto Lingüístico de Verano.

——. 1968d. Titæ. Giqueta apænekã, Waorani. Quito: Instituto Lingüístico de Verano.

——. 1975. Leyenda de la viejita que rejuveneció, según la versión del tío Giquita (Spanish and English versions). Quito: Instituto Lingüístico de Verano.

—— and Kenneth L. Pike. 1959. Notas sobre fonémica huaorani (auca). Estudios acerca de las lenguas huaorani (auca), shimigáe, y zápara. Publiciones científicas del Ministerio de Educación del Ecuador 4–17.

—— and ——. 1962. Auca Phonemics. Studies in Ecuadorian Indian Languages 1:2–30. The Summer Institute of Linguistics Publications in Linguistics and Related Fields 7.

Schram, Judith L. and Linda K. Jones. 1979. Participant reference in narrative discourse in Mazatec of Jalapa de Díaz. In Linda K. Jones (ed), Discourse Studies in Mesoamerican Languages 1.269–89. Summer Institute of Linguistics and the University of Texas at Arlington Publications in Linguistics 58.

Schram, Terry L. 1979. Tense, tense embedding and theme in discourse in Mazatec of Jalapa de Díaz. In Linda K. Jones (ed), Discourse Studies in Mesoamerican Languages 1.141–67. The Summer Institute of Linguistics and the University of Texas at Arlington Publications in Linguistics 58.

Thomas, Dorothy. 1978. The discourse level in Chrau. Mon Khmer studies 7.233–95. Honolulu: The University of Hawaii.

van Dijk, Teun. 1972. Some aspects of text grammars. The Hague: Mouton.

Wallis, Ethel Emily. [1960] 1965. The Dayuma Story. New York: Harper and Row.

———. 1973. Aucas Downriver: Dayuma's story today. New York: Harper and Rowe.

Walrod, Michael R. 1979. Discourse grammar in Ga'dang. Summer Institute of Linguistics and the University of Texas at Arlington Publications in Linguistics 63.

Wise, Mary Ruth. 1963. Six levels of structure in Amuesha (Arawak) verbs. International Journal of American Linguistics 29:132–52.

———. [1968] 1971. Identification of participants in discourse: a study of aspects of form and meaning in Nomatsiquenga. Summer Institute of Linguistics Publications in Linguistics and Related Fields 28.

Part I

Some Grammatical Structures of Discourse

What Can Mark the Peak of a Story?
Michael Miller

[Languages usually mark the high point of excitement or the most important point of a discourse with a special grammatical structure. Waorani discourse follows this pattern, employing several peak-marking devices. These devices are here classified according to Longacre's (1976b:217-29) typology of peak markers. There appears to be no single preferred type of peak marker in this language. One device is the use of rhetorical underlining, characterized by the paraphrasing or repetition of the main point of a story. Other devices are a shift from narrative to drama or from history to narrative genre, role reversal, or change-of-pace in the form of unusually long sentences.]

Good authors and storytellers are often judged to be so by their ability to build suspense in a story in a masterful way. Once suspense is at a high point, the storyteller resolves the tension with an equally masterful touch. The point at which suspense is at its peak is called by many literary critics the CLIMAX. This climax is often marked by one or another stylistic device that sets it apart from the body of the story. Borrowing terminology from Robert Longacre (1976a:216-17), such devices can be called PEAK MARKERS. The sentence or construction where the climax occurs can be called the PEAK of the story.

1. Theoretical background. Longacre (1976b:216) says that peak refers "to any episode-like unit set apart by special surface structure features and corresponding to the climax or denouement in the deep structure." He has further classified these surface structures into several categories which will be described briefly, since they are essential to the understanding of this paper.

But before these peak markers are described, it is important to note that, although peak markers are found in narrative discourse, a narrative discourse does not always have a single peak. Rather than having a climax that is marked in the surface structure, a narrative may consist of a number of episodes combined into one story with a central theme. Longacre (1976b:218) mentions that he thinks Dicken's *Great Expectations* is such a novel. Longacre (1976b:213) also mentions that the type of peak-marking devices discussed in this paper apply primarily to climactic narrative discourse. He mentions, however, that other discourse genres besides narrative have something analogous to peak. This includes hortatory, expository, and procedural genres. The peaks in these other genres can be marked by some of the same devices that mark peak in climactic narrative genre, as will be seen.

The first of the peak-marking devices is called RHETORICAL UNDERLINING (Longacre 1976b:217). The basic idea here is that an author will use words during the climax of a narrative in order to mark that climax. These word complexes may take several forms. They may be seen, for example, as repetition, or as paraphrase, in which an event may be looked at from different perspectives.

HEIGHTENED VIVIDNESS is the name given to a second type of peak marker (Longacre 1976b:219). There are three different ways in which this type of marker is seen in the surface structure of a narrative. First, a tense shift may be used to bring about a heightened vividness. This may be seen in a switch from past tense to present tense at the climax of the narrative. Longacre (1976b:219) mentions the example of a story from the Fore language where this type of peak marker is seen. The story starts out in the far past tense. As the story continues and the plot becomes more involved, the tense changes to the recent past. At the climax of the story, there is a shift into the present tense. After this, the story shifts back into the far past tense for the conclusion.

A second device for bringing about heightened vividness is to shift reference to a certain individual in the narrative from a less-specific to a more-specific person marker. A story that starts out in the third person, for example, might shift to first person at its climax.

A third device for heightening vividness involves a CHANGE IN NARRATIVE STYLE. This change (which Longacre calls a shift schema) is a progression from a narrative style, to a pseudodialogue style, to a dialogue style, and finally to a drama style. Such a story is still a narrative, but the specific speech or writing style goes through this progression (Longacre 1976b:221). This shift draws the reader or listener into the story. An example would be a story which starts as being reported by a third party who first appears to be absent from the event, but suddenly speaks as though being present (compare Longacre 1976b:225).

A change in the size of grammatical constructions, or the number of connective words used, are also devices that Longacre (1976b:223–25) mentions as peak-marking devices. He calls this type a CHANGE OF PACE, since that is the effect these devices have on the progression of the story. They can either speed up an event line or slow it down. (By event line, I mean the sequence of main events of the story over a period of time.)

A peak may be marked by a CHANGE IN ORIENTATION. The predominate subject of the story, furthermore, can become at the climax, its object. Many times this takes the form of the initial victim in a story becoming the first overcomer (Longacre 1976b:227). It is sometimes realized by an inanimate object becoming the grammatical subject at the peak of a story.

Longacre (1976b:217) says that these devices are like a bag of tricks that a narrator can draw upon to mark a peak. Jones and Jones (1979:19) suggest that some languages may have PREFERRED devices for marking peak. They cite several examples of languages that use either one of the previously mentioned devices exclusively, or some other device to mark peak in the surface structure of the discourse. They say, for example, that Lachixio Zapotec typically marks peak by the use of sentences which are very long and contain many clauses in comparison to the other sentences in the discourse (Jones and Jones 1979:20).

2. Methodology. I have attempted to discover some peak markers of Waorani discourse and to see whether some are preferred over others. The following methodology was used. Six Waorani texts were analyzed. First, what appeared to be the intended climax of each story was postulated after reading the free translation of the discourse, and looking at some Waorani texts. Next, these hypotheses about the presence of a climax were checked with Rachel Saint, who had recorded and transcribed the texts and who has been a student of the language for nearly twenty years. After this, the Waorani transcriptions were checked for occurrences of any of the previously mentioned peak-marking devices, plus any other special markers that might be noticed. The final step was to make decisions concerning which devices were actually being used.

3. Analysis. The first text examined is entitled 'The Origin of the Rainbow'. It is a story of nine sentences about what should and should not be done when the rainbow is seen.

This story would probably be classified as hortatory by Longacre. The methods of marking peak mentioned above apply primarily to climactic narrative genre discourse; but Longacre (1976b:229) says that hortatory can have a peak, which he basically equates with the main point that the speaker is trying to get across.

In this story, the first seven lines are exhortations of the elders regarding rainbows. The last two sentences are comparable to an illustration in a sermon. They show what happened to Waorani people who followed the exhortations.

There seem to be two main points made in the exhortations. The most important of these is found in sentence 1, which says that the Waorani people should go to the end of the rainbow for the best clay. There is evidence for rhetorical underlining here. Sentences 1 and 6–9 all speak to the point; and sentences 8 and 9 appear to be the most vivid of the discourse, since they are in narrative genre. Sentence 6 is the longest sentence of the discourse. It reiterates the exhortation that the people should go to the place where the rainbow touches the ground, in order to find the best clay. It was probably on the basis of these features that I decided sentence 6 is the peak. In addition, the end of the text mentions only that the Waorani people found the good clay. The second point, in sentences 2–5, is advice against pointing at rainbows; this might lead to the paralysis of a person's arm.

The second discourse looked at is called 'The Origin of Cassava for Food'. It has thirty-eight sentences and is basically a procedural discourse. Longacre (1976b:228) says that a target procedure takes the place of the climax and of the denouement in procedural discourse. The target procedure in this discourse is how to prepare cassava for food. The actual instructions begin in sentence 12 and go through sentence 18. This is the peak of the discourse. It is marked by a shift from narrative to drama genre (Longacre 1976b). The cassava speaks directly to the hunter in sentences 12 through 18. In sentence 19 the hunter replies. Then there is a shift back to narrative style. Sentence 23 shifts back into pseudodialogue and then sentence 24 to drama. This second shift could be called the denouement.

'The Jaguar and the Turtle' story, with fifty-eight sentences, is the third discourse examined. It is the story of a baby turtle threatened by a jaguar who has plans to eat him. The turtle outwits the jaguar, kills him, and then shows his accomplishment to the Waorani, who take the teeth and claws of the jaguar for use as decorations.

The peak of the story occurs at sentence 23. Up to this point, the jaguar is the aggressor, the turtle the victim. Now, the turtle becomes the aggressor and the jaguar the victim. This role reversal is one of the characteristics which Longacre calls CHANGE OF ORIENTATION. Another peak-marking device also shows up at this same point in the narrative. Sentence 23 is by far the longest sentence in the narrative. It is twenty-seven words long. The next longest sentences, 21 and 44, are sixteen words long. This long sentence is characteristic of change-of-pace peak marking and seems to serve this purpose here.

The next story, 'The Alligator and the Bird', is a narrative of fifty sentences which tells about a bird that played a prank on an alligator. The bird talked the alligator into making an agreement with him that neither would eat anything. The bird, however, would dart off to eat every time the alligator fell asleep. Not knowing this, the alligator continued with the agreement until he almost starved. Eventually, he becomes suspicious and discovers the bird's perfidy.

The point at which the alligator becomes suspicious is the beginning of the peak of this story. In sentence 35, the alligator begins to wonder what is going on and decides to find out. Sentence 36 says that the alligator pretended to be asleep but surreptitiously watched the bird. Sentences 37 through 40 tell of his discovery that the bird was not keeping his word and of the alligator's subsequent angry tirade. This is a type of paraphrase—a sign that rhetorical underlining is being used.

The next discourse analyzed is called 'The Spider Monkey's Tail'. It is a narrative about how the Waorani people dealt with the menace of the spider monkey, also telling something of the habits of this monkey. There are twenty-one sentences. The basic plot is as follows: The Waorani people are attacked by the spider monkey when they go swimming. He pulls them under the water by wrapping his tail around their necks, and drowns them. One of the Waorani people decides he will fight back. He devises a plan and the next time the spider monkey tries to drown one of the Waorani people, the man cuts off the monkey's tail. From then on, the Waorani people have no problem dealing with spider monkeys.

The peak of this story seems to begin at sentence 9 and goes through sentence 13. Suspense in the story is built up by previous descriptions of Waorani people being drowned by the spider monkey. The Waorani people realize that if this keeps up, they all will eventually be drowned. At sentence 8 we have the beginning of a change in roles. Prior to this point in the narrative, the Waorani people are the victims of the spider monkey's designs. They are primarily the undergoers of the action in the narrative up to this point. In sentence 9, however, one of the Waorani people says, "Now I am going to cut off his tail." From this point on, the Waorani people become primarily agents of the action and the spider monkey becomes the undergoer. This role reversal is an evidence of a change-of-orientation peak marking.

There is another important surface structure feature at this point in the narrative. Sentence 11 is almost twice as long as any of the other sentences in the discourse. It has thirty words. The next longest sentences are 6 and 1. They have seventeen and fifteen words, respectively. This run-on sentence is a clear indication of change-of-pace peak marking.

The final discourse that was analyzed is called 'The Spider Monkey's Thumbs'. It is a very short narrative discourse of seventeen sentences which tells how the spider monkey came to have no thumbs. At one time, spider monkeys did have thumbs, according to the storyteller. They used to eat jungle grapes that lay on the ground. Then they tried to get grapes in the trees. When the monkeys on the ground tried to catch a bunch of grapes which the monkeys in the trees threw to them, their thumbs were knocked off. From then on, spider monkeys just had four fingers and no thumbs.

The peak of this story seems to begin at sentence 8 and goes through sentence 11. Sentence 8 is the one where a spider monkey tried to catch the grapes and his thumbs were knocked off. Sentences 9 through 16 paraphrase that thought, with the exception of sentence 12, which is a type of denouement. It states that the spider monkeys never had thumbs after they were knocked off that first time.

Chronological and Logical Discourse Chains
Deborah Ross

[Just as individual links of metal are put together to form a chain, sentences in the Waorani language are often linked together to form a chain of sentences. In the texts examined, chaining most frequently serves as a chronological link, denoting either a sequential or simultaneous occurrence of events. Less frequently a chain serves as a logical link between events. Chains usually occur within the boundaries of the paragraph, unifying the information within.]

In Waorani discourse sentences are often linked together by a mechanism called a chain. Longacre describes how chaining works: "The device basically consists in repeating, paraphrasing, or referring in some manner at the onset of a succeeding sentence to the whole or part of the preceding sentence" (Longacre 1968:56). The purpose of this paper is to describe the various roles of verb chaining in Waorani discourse, although other types of chaining also occur in the Waorani language and may have the same roles as verb chaining.

1. Sentence, clause, and verb structure. As a background to the grammatical structure of a chain, it is important to understand Waorani sentence, clause, and verb structure. The most common Waorani sentence is composed of one or more premarginal dependent clauses with the role of circumstance or sequence, and a nuclear independent clause with the role of proposition. A rough formula follows.

Common Sentence = ±	PreMar	Dep Cl	Nuc	Ind Cl
	Circumstance Sequence	——	+ Prop	——

At least seven basic clause types have tentatively been defined. They are transitive, speech transitive, bitransitive, intransitive, identitive, equative, and biintransitive—all of which may be chained.

Dependency and independency are contrasted at the verb level, usually by a mode, aspect, or limit marker.

Independent
(mode) -pa
(mode) ∅ (with no limit
    or aspect marker)

Dependent
(mode) -te
(limit -ke
among other meanings)
(aspect) -ñõ-

2. Chain structure. A typical Waorani chain consists of at least two sentences. The first sentence (sentence 1) has an independent clause (Clause A) in its nuclear slot. The second sentence (sentence 2) is composed of a dependent clause (Clause B) in the premarginal slot and an independent clause (Clause C) in the nuclear slot. Clause A contains information that is new. Clause B repeats some or all of the information from Clause A; this information is now old information. Clause B may also contain new information in addition to the repeated information. Completely new information is given in Clause C. This is illustrated as follows:

Sentence 1	Sentence 2	
Clause A	Clause B	Clause C
Independent	Dependent	Independent
new info	old info	new info
51. tǽnõ-nãni-ta-pa spear-3p-pst-asser They speared him.	52. tǽnõ-te spearing Spearing him,	õta baga ǽǽ-nãni-ta-pa claw teeth take-3p-pst-asser they took the claws and teeth.

The grammatical elements repeated in Clause B are primarily the verb or verb phrase along with undergoer, scope, and marginal words.

The illustration above shows one link of a chain. It is possible to continue the chain by continuing to repeat information from consecutive clauses. If a, b, c, d, e, . . . are pieces of information, they would be chained as follows: a, ab, bc, cd, de, ... In several Waorani texts, examples of three, four, and five chained sentences have been found.

Verb chaining seems to be a frequently used linking device in most of the Waorani texts used for this study. Occurrence of chains in the six texts are listed below:

Text	Chains	Sentences
The Origin of the Rainbow	1	9
The Origin of Cassava	7	38
The Jaguar and the Turtle	12	58
The Origin of the Corn-Bees	8	18
The Spider Monkey's Tail	4	21
The Spider Monkey's Thumbs	1	17

Chaining occurs most frequently in the Origin of the Corn-Bees—in almost half of the sentences of the text. Narrative style lends itself to chaining, and this particular text contains longer stretches of uninterrupted narration than the other texts.

The basic function of chaining in the Waorani language is linkage of events. Clause B links Clause A and Clause C together. This linkage is of two types—chronological and logical.

3. Chronological linkage. Chaining can serve to link two or more events in time. It can show SEQUENTIAL occurrence (event A happened before event B happened) or it can show simultaneous occurrence (event A happened at the same time as event B). In OC 14–15, event A happens first; event B happens second.

Event A:
  14. *Botō yæwa mānī ōŋipodē ǣ wogabi.*
  Pull up my root from the ground.

Sequential Link:
  15. *ǣ wogabi ate*
  Having pulled me up,

Event B:
  æǣ-te gobi.
  take me with you.

The verb *ate* 'seeing' often appears in the linking clause, its presence usually indicating a sequential relationship between clauses.

In JT 16–17, two events occur SIMULTANEOUSLY–the turtle swings in his hammock while the jaguar approaches. Here we have simple chaining. The first verb is repeated, without tense or independent mode-marking suffix.

Event A:
  16. *Ñōōmēnē kæwokātapa titæke.*
  Little turtle swung in his hammock.

Simultaneous Link:
   17. *Kæwokã̄,*
   While swinging,

Event B:
   mẽñe, Guĩnẽ takabi aboe.
   Jaguar said: "Stick out your head so I can see it."

The aspect marker *ñõ* often appears in the linking clause to indicate simultaneous occurrence of events; it is translated 'while'. An example of this is found in JT 3–4.

Event A:
   3. The great big jaguar was coming closer and closer.

Simultaneous Link:
   4. *Owiya(a)ke põñõŋa*
   While he was coming across the ridge,

Event B:
   the little turtle was swinging in his hammock slung in a field of tree stumps.

4. Logical linkage. Chaining also functions in Waorani as a LOGICAL LINK between two or more events. One example of logical linkage is found in OR 2–3.

Event A Cause:
   2. *Oo kæmõnãmaĩ.*
   Don't point at it.

Logical Link:
   3. *Oo kæmõte ate,*
   If you point at it,

Event B Effect:
   õnõmæ̃ kæpæ̃te bakæb(i)ĩpa.
   your arm will become paralyzed.

The logical relationship between these two events is one of cause and effect. Pointing at the rainbow will cause your arm to become paralyzed. The cause-effect relationship is also seen in OC 37. The fact that they had taken the cassava (event A) caused the tapir to cry (event B).

Event A Cause:
> 37. *Tõmē ēkayǣ go tōmāā ǣǣnānitapa.*
> Later he went, they had taken all (the cassava).

Logical Link:
> *kǣnǣ ǣmǣwo ǣǣnāni ate,*
> Seeing they had taken the last cassava roots,

Event B Effect:
> *titǣ botō kēwē āte wiyǣ wiyǣ wǣgat(e)ĩpa.*
> the tapir cried, Ĩt was my cassava, boo hoo, boo hoo."

5. Linkage within a paragraph. Sentences within a paragraph of a discourse may be linked chronologically, logically, or both, by verb chaining. In the narrative the Origin of Cassava, sentences 23 through 29 comprise a monologue by the cassava plant. The main criterion for determining paragraph boundaries here is speaker change. Within this monologue there is some type of marked linkage between each sentence, with one exception. There is no marked linkage between 23 and 24, but this is possibly due to the fact that sentence 23 is an introductory sentence and does not need to be linked into the rest of the paragraph. Sentences 24 through 29 are linked by one of three devices—verb chaining, *ayǣ* 'then', or *ate* 'seeing'. The linking mechanisms for this paragraph are shown below.

Linkage:	English Translation:
Introduction	"This is what you must do to me," the Cassava Plant said. "Break off my stalk.
ayǣ	Then after you have chopped down the trees and cleared away the weeds, plant me and let me grow.
chain	When it grows, and you see I have leaves, don't take me yet.
ayǣ	Just wait until all the leaves are grown,
ayǣ	then clear the weeds, and when you see that the cassava in the ground right there humps up the earth,
ayǣ	then dig up the cassava root, take it,
ayǣ	and eat it.
chain	Eat it like that,
ayǣ	then plant me on the other clearings farther and farther away. I'll grow and, eating cassava, you will live."

6. The absence of chaining. Grimes (1975:96) says, "In a system that makes extensive use of linkages, it is the absence of a linking clause that catches the hearer's attention. This break in the system may be used to signal a change of scene or a shift of participants or a transition to background information or even a point of special emphasis." In the Waorani texts studied, it has been found that a break in a long chain does in fact sometimes signal changes like those mentioned by Grimes. In the narrative Origin of the Corn-Bees, a long sequence of events is linked primarily by chaining. The linkage is broken near the end of the narrative with a simple sentence. At this point the chain is broken. The preceding sentences have been complex, made up of dependent and independent clauses and a 'rhythm' has been established by the chaining device. The unlinked simple sentence catches the hearer's attention and seems to put special emphasis on the information. This sentence also introduces a new participant—the Corn-Bees. Since the purpose of the narrator is to tell the origin of the Corn-Bees, this sentence is highlighted by a break in linkage and does in fact introduce the story topic, the arrival of the Corn-Bees.

Linkage:	English Translation:
	One fellow chopped a corn field; he chopped a whole great big field for corn.
chain	He chopped it and had lots of corn growing, so much it grew like cane in a cane-patch.
chain	They said, "When your corn is grown and we see it is ripe and you are eating it, let us eat it too."
neg link	But he replied, "Since you refused to share with me and ate all your corn, I refuse too.
ate	When the corn is ripe, all alone I will eat it up. In one day I am going to gobble it all up."
chain	Then one day the corn tassles became dark.
chain	When the tassles became dark the fellow ate his corn in one day.
Narrator's comment	The rascal! When the firewood was piled on the ground-fire, he cooked it all.
chain	He acted as if he were starved.
chain	As if he were starved, he ate lots and lots of corn.
chain	And having eaten so much, his insides suddenly swelled and burst open.
chain	Having swelled and burst open, the contents of his stomach spilled out.
break-in chain–topic	The corn-Bees buzzed and buzzed around there.

Hypothesis on Helping to Identify Waorani Discourse Types

Carol Hepner

[Suffixes help to identify the kind of discourse a text is. Preliminary analysis suggests that the past tense identifies a legend; the future tense a discourse of instructions. The lack or infrequent use of a tense suffix seems to identify a discourse which gives advice.]

In the Waorani language, a verb suffix marks the tense of an action. These suffixes help to identify what kind of discourse a text is. Each type of discourse seems to have a certain tense that is most commonly connected with it. Some criteria used to determine what tense is characteristic of a certain discourse are the frequency of occurrence of a tense and the type of information conveyed by a tense. One kind of discourse is a legend or folktale. These use the past tense most frequently. In one legend, the Alligator and the Bird story, only one sentence does not use the past tense. This sentence occurs right at the beginning of the story when the bird suggests a contest in which he and the alligator will not eat for two years. The rest of the story uses the past tense to tell how the bird tricked the alligator so that the alligator almost died. The frequent use of the past tense helps to identify the Alligator and the Bird story as a legend.

Another type of discourse is one that gives instructions on how to do something. The Origin of Cassava is such a discourse. Although the future tense is not the most frequently used tense, it conveys the most important information. The crucial instructions given to the hunter concerning how to plant and cook cassava are given in the future tense. The actions of the hunter in following the instructions are given in another tense. The use of the future tense helps to identify the Origin of Cassava as a discourse that gives instructions.

A third kind of text to be considered is one that gives advice. In the Origin of the Rainbow, only one of the verbs is marked with a tense suffix. The infrequency of the occurrence of any tense helps to identify this text as one that gives advice; the advice concerns where to find good clay and how to point at the rainbow. The advice is permanently applicable; it does not require time orientation.

The Function of ayǣ 'then' in Waorani

Mary E. Holman

[Two of the important functions of *ayǣ* are to mark result and important instructions on the discourse level. *Ayǣ* functions differently in procedural and hortatory discourse than it does in narrative discourse. In procedural and hortatory discourse it marks important instructions, while in all three types of discourse it marks result. *Ayǣ* often indicates relative chronology at the same time that it marks result and instructions.]

The purpose of this paper is to present the functions of the word *ayǣ* 'then' in Waorani discourse. My original hypothesis was that *ayǣ* functioned in discourse to mark significant events, the peak of the discourse, or important participants of its referential hierarchy. When I was unable to substantiate this hypothesis in all the texts, I began studying the grammatical structure of the discourses and discovered that the predominant function of *ayǣ* is to mark result. Another important function of *ayǣ* is to mark crucial instructions in procedural and hortatory discourse. Overlapping with these two functions is its role as a subsequent time relator.

The three texts which I studied most extensively are the Origin of the Rainbow (OR), the Origin of Cassava for Food (OC), both told by Dayuma, and the Jaguar and the Turtle (JT) as told by Giketa. I also studied The Spider Monkey's Tail (TL), The Spider Monkey's Thumbs (TH), and The Alligator and the Bird (AB), all told by Giketa.

This paper is divided into three major parts based upon three functions of *ayǣ*. The first part discusses the use of *ayǣ* to mark important instructions, the second part discusses the use of *ayǣ* to mark result, and the third part discusses the use of *ayǣ* to indicate relative time.

1. The use of ayǣ to mark important instructions. According to Longacre (1976b:199), procedural and hortatory discourse tell us how something is done or how we should act, respectively. The Origin of Cassava for Food is a procedural discourse and The Origin of the Rainbow is a hortatory discourse. *Ayǣ* has a function in procedural and hortatory discourse that it does not have in narrative discourse. In procedural and hortatory discourse it marks the instructions.

In The Origin of the Rainbow, *ayǽ* occurs only four times. The first three occurrences of *ayǽ* mark the important instructions in the story. *Ayǽ* is used twice to highlight a prohibition against pointing at the rainbow.

OR 2 *Ayǽ Oo kǽmōnāmaī.*
       Then they said, "Don't point at it."

OR 5 *Ayǽ ōnōpo īte oo kǽdāmaī.*
       Be sure you never point with your hand.

Then *ayǽ* marks the main point of the text, which is the instructions of how to find the best clay to make pots.

OR 6 *Ayǽ tōmēñōmō ǽdōnō ōŋīpo pō, tōmēñōmō kǽyǽ gobi, dai ate, wa(a)ēmō dai kǽyǽ bækū bakǽīpa.*
       Then, wherever it touches the earth, quickly go there to that place; whatever clay you see there will surely be the best clay for making pots.

The Origin of Cassava is a text that is much longer than the Origin of the Rainbow. In The Origin of Cassava, *ayǽ* is used extensively to mark important instructions. The Cassava Plant gives two sets of instructions. The first set is to take the cassava, cook it, and eat it. *Ayǽ* marks each of these commands.

OC 12–13 *Ayǽ Kēwē, Botō īmote ǽǣŋīm(i)īpa.*
           Then the Cassava Plant spoke to him, "Take me;"

OC 16b *ayǽ wēte kǽgadēnǽ ǽnōŋīm(i)īpa*
         cook the inside part of the cassava;

OC 17 *ayǽ kǽŋīm(i)īpa.*
        then eat it.

The second important set of instructions is to cut the weeds and plant the cassava, let it grow leaves, cut back the weeds, let the cassava mature, dig it up, eat some of it, then plant some of it further away. Each of these instructions is also marked by *ayǽ*.

OC 25 *Ayǽ ōmæ wiyæbi awǽ yite ate mīmi pǽkāe.*
        Then after you have chopped down the trees and cleared away the weeds, plant me and let me grow;

OC 27a *Ayæ e ai, tōmāā ēēke ōñabo babo ayæ ōmæ wibi, ...*
Just wait until all the leaves are grown, then clear the weeds, ...

OC 28 *Ayæ kænæ wogakīm(i)īpa, æǣŋīm(i)īpa, ayæ kæ̃ŋīm(i)īpa.*
Then dig up the cassava root, take it, and eat it.

OC 29b *. . . ayæ wayōmō wayōmō gabi.*
. . . then plant me on clearings farther and farther away."

The instructions marked by *ayæ* are the core of the Cassava Plant's instructions in The Origin of Cassava.

2. The use of ayæ to mark result. In procedural and hortatory discourse, the use of *ayæ* to mark result, and the use of *ayæ* to mark important instructions, are closely related. *Ayæ* sometimes marks the result of following the instructions.

A characteristic of *ayæ* which was helpful in determining its function as a result marker is that it usually occurs with a clause which has an independent verb. It does this unambiguously several times in The Origin of Cassava.

OC 30 *Ao āte, īmai ātapa āte, æǣte mao awæ yite gakātapa ayæ pæpa.*
"OK, I'll do what I was told," he decided. So he took the cassava, chopped down the trees, planted it, and it grew.

OC 31 *Ōmæ wikā, ayæ kænæ ēwapa bapa.*
He cleared the weeds, then the cassava root formed.

Because of this characteristic, in several places where it was not clear whether *ayæ* referred to an independent or a dependent clause, I chose to relate it to the independent clause, thus clarifying its function as a result marker. For example, in sentences 33 and 34 of The Origin of Cassava, it is at first unclear whether *ayæ* marks the root becoming big, or the hunter eating it. (But cf. p.20, second paragraph.)

OC 33-34 *Ayæ ñǣnæ bawa, Mānōmaī ātapa, āte, kæ̃ŋātapa.*
"Then the root became big." That's what the Cassava Plant said to me. "When it's like that, it's mature." So he ate it.

By applying this principle in OC 34 (noting the independent verb *kæ̃ŋātapa* 'he ate'), I was able to determine that *ayæ* referred to the hunter eating the cassava, which is a result of the whole process of the cassava plant growing.

In The Origin of the Rainbow, the first three occurrences of *ayæ̃* mark important instructions. The final *ayæ̃* marks the result of following those instructions.

OR 9 *Ayæ̃ waa kæ̃yæ̃ bæte kĕwĕnãnipa.*
Then, using it, they made clay pots.

In The Origin of Cassava, there are two sets of instructions given by the Cassava Plant. Four things happened as a result of the hunter following all of these instructions: (1) the cassava plant grew, (2) the cassava plant formed, (3) the cassava plant was still immature, and (4) when it became big, then the hunter ate it. *Ayæ̃* marks all of these clauses. Note that each of the first three clauses follows an action by the hunter and that the final *ayæ̃* introduces the result of the whole process—the cassava became big and the hunter ate it.

OC 30 *Ao ãte, ĩmaĩ ãtapa ãte, æǽte mao awæ̃ yite gakãtapa ayæ̃ pæpa*
"OK. I'll do what I was told," he decided. So he took the cassava, chopped down the trees, planted it, and it grew;

OC 31 *Õõmæ wikã, ayæ̃ kæ̃nǽ ẽwapa bapa.*
'He cleared the weeds; then the cassava root formed;'

OC 32 *Wædǽke wogate akã ayæ̃ wẽẽñǽnǽ ĩpa.*
He dug up a little to see. It was still not fully developed.

OC 33 *Ayæ̃ ñǽnǽ bawa,*
Then the root became big;

OC 34 *Mãnõmaĩ ãtapa, ãte, kǽŋãtapa*
That's what the Cassava Plant said to me. "When it's like that, it's mature." So he ate it.

Narrative discourse recounts events (Longacre 1976b:199). *Ayæ̃* can mark result in narrative discourse as well as in procedural and hortatory discourse. In The Origin of Cassava, the procedural discourse is embedded in narrative discourse. *Ayæ̃* marks a result (1) in the last sentence of the narrative discourse which comes before the embedded procedural discourse, and (2) in the first sentence of the narrative discourse which follows the embedded procedural discourse. Preceding the Cassava Plant's instructions, the hunter is puzzling over the tapir tracks. When he goes again to find out why there are so many, then (as a result of going) he sees that many tapirs live there beside the cassava patch.

OC 11 *Ayǣ gote ædǣmō titæ nāŋī nāŋī nāŋī kōwē kěwē kěwē weka*
Then going and looking carefully he saw that lots and lots and lots of tapirs lived right there beside the cassava patch.

After the hunter had followed the Cassava Plant's instructions, the cassava had grown, and the hunter had eaten the cassava, then the hunter called his friends to see this good thing.

OC 35-36 *Ayǣ wadāni ĩnānite, Pō aidāni, titæ kěwē waa ǣǣtabopa.*
Then he called to the others, "Come see! I happily took the tapir's cassava."

The Jaguar and the Turtle is a narrative discourse. In this text, there are only four occurrences of *ayǣ*. Three of them occur immediately following the peak of the story. In the peak, the jaguar opened his mouth and the turtle jumped in and began biting the jaguar inside his throat. The result, marked by three occurrences of *ayǣ*, is that the jaguar fell down, the jaguar remained down, and the turtle crawled out.

JT 26 *Ayǣ æo æo æo pokǣñōŋā měñe wæǣŋā.*
Then, as he kept biting him, the jaguar fell down.

JT 27 *Tǣ. Æbānō wǣŋātawo āte, ayǣ ega ega měñe doobæ wæǣte ōñōŋā.*
Plunk! The little turtle wondered if he were really dead, but the jaguar was still thrashing after he fell and lay on the ground.

JT 28 *Ayǣ ega titæke daa godō ti.*
Then he wiggled again, and the turtle crawled out and dropped to the ground.

The final occurrence of *ayǣ* in The Jaguar and the Turtle introduces the result of the Waorani's hearing the turtle's story. Because the turtle said it was true, the Waorani followed his trail to the dead jaguar.

JT 44 *Ānānike Doo nawāŋapōni āŋā ĩnānike, ayǣ tōměŋā nānō godō giidāmǣ tao, giidāmǣ tao, ōnōke wa(a)ěmōmōni ěā ōñō.*
Since the little turtle said it was true, they followed his trail going around and around the stumps, to where the beautiful jaguar lay.

3. The use of *ayǣ* to indicate relative time. The third function of *ayǣ* usually overlaps with the first two. Instructions which *ayǣ* highlights in

The Origin of Cassava follow one another in time. It is also typical that results which *ayǣ* marks tend to follow in time the events which bring them about. The instructions in The Origin of the Rainbow— 'Don't point at it' and 'Go toward the rainbow'—could prove either simultaneous in time or subsequent in time.

Occasionally *ayǣ* relates subsequent time without marking result or instructions. In The Alligator and the Bird, the first *ayǣ* to be used indicates that the event which it introduces comes after the preceding one, without stipulating result or instructions. It is used in AB 11 to show the sequence of the alligator's checking on the bird, after AB 10 in which he sleeps intermittently, merely seeing the bird between naps.

AB 10 *Itǣdē woyowotǣ ñāni omǣmōte ad(ē)īke a, mō ñōŋā.*
Whenever he woke up by night or day he looked up and saw the bird just sitting on the limb, so he went to sleep again.

AB 11 *Ayǣ, ǣbānō biwii kǣkātawo āte, nōma ñāni ōmǣmōte ǣmō akā.*
Every time the alligator woke up he looked up saying, "I wonder how the little bird is doing."

Conclusion. In order to analyze the function of *ayǣ* 'then' in the Waorani language, it is necessary to study its role above the sentence level in the grammatical structure, and in relation to genre discourse.

Thematic Unity as Evidence for the Presence of Paragraphs

Mark Hepner

[An analysis of several Waorani texts suggests that a clustering of sentences around a theme demonstrates the existence of the paragraph as a level intermediate between sentence and discourse. Some grammatical clues join with theme to help support this conclusion.]

My particular interest in studying Waorani stories was to try to determine two things: (1) What are the linguistic criteria for determining the existence of paragraphs within a story and (2) can Waorani stories be divided into paragraphs by means of such criteria.

Being able to identify paragraphs is important for several reasons. First of all, paragraphs organize stories into manageable chunks which a reader or hearer can handle more easily than the entire story all at once. Secondly, paragraphs help a reader or hearer keep track of where he is in the story. Paragraphs help to convey the full import of a message by reducing confusion or distortion which could result without such organization.

After surveying some of the literature (Beekman and Callow 1979:82; Grimes 1975:35–36, 103, 107–09, 114, 358; Halliday and Hasan 1976:1–2; Jones 1977:1–2, 6, 130–31, 224–61, 225, 260; Longacre 1976a:276, 1976b:169, 1979:116–18, 276; Peeke 1973; Pike and Pike 1977:25, 262; Van Dijk 1976), I feel that thematic unity is the most important characteristic of paragraphs. Theme, as we were taught in high school and college, is the most important concept found in such units of speech.

Themes tend to organize stories into clusters of sentences. I decided that if I could find the themes of Waorani stories, then I could expect to find such sentence clusterings and, therefore, paragraphs. Further study revealed that there are specific clues which enable a reader or hearer to discern the themes of a particular story. These clues are grammatical marking, repetition, and the general-to-specific criterion.

The most obvious instance of grammatical marking is that the theme of each paragraph is stated in the first sentence of that paragraph. If a new character or idea is to be developed over a sequence of sentences, it is always stated in the first sentence of that sequence.

Repetition is another clue to the identification of the themes of a story. In the Jaguar and the Turtle story, the jaguar repeatedly asks the turtle where his mother and father are. This emphasis on the turtle not having parents marks the theme of this paragraph as the turtle's orphanhood.

The general-to-specific criterion also may identify the type of theme which is in view. The most general theme, which includes the entire story, is called the global theme; the specific themes, restricted to just one paragraph, are local themes.

With the help of these clues, Waorani stories were divided into sections composed of clusters of sentences which developed local themes and could be called paragraphs.

Part II

Some Grammatical Structures from Discourse to Morpheme Classes

Some Grammatical Structures from Discourse to Morpheme Classes

We turn from general structure to grammatical detail, and from TELLING ABOUT to FINDING OUT ABOUT. Eventually, a clear understanding of a grammatical structure must rest upon methods for finding out what that structure is—although such methods and preliminary materials are often not published, but may be deduced, in part, only by implication from the elegantly-polished end products of that grinding search.

In this part of the presentation, we attempt to show how some of the data, for a language previously unknown to an investigator, can be made to surrender grammatical secrets. The reader interested only in final results, who never expects to face such a situation, might choose to skip hurriedly over these charts and trees, even though fruit grows on their branches and twigs.

We are here dealing with the structure of the way a story is actually told—not the way it might be paraphrased or told with other emphases or with a different selection of data. We are dealing here, in our terms, with grammar rather than with referential structure. And this telling structure differs from language to language, from genre to genre, from total text down to chapters, paragraphs, clauses, phrases, words, and classes of lexical bits. A tree diagram of a text shows some components of the structures which make up that text. But the single tree can neither show (1) the variety of variants of those structures, with their optional or obligatory parts, or order of parts, nor (2) optional or obligatory variants in terms of classes of items filling their various slots. In this sense, any tree representation is in part etic. One who wishes an emic representation, must move to the use of formulas which show such variants.

A preliminary analysis of the grammar of the texts is given first, in the first article of this section, for all levels of two texts. Then a sample formulaic emic development is given for clause, in the second article, and for verb structures in the third.

Two theoretical principles of importance must be kept in mind as one reads this material, if one wishes to understand the motivation underlying it.

(1) The grammatical and referential hierarchies, as just implied above, are considered to be separate but simultaneous structurings of a stream of speech. (The phonological structuring is a third.) The grammatical structure is linear—the structural order and pattern in which a story is told or in which orders are given. It is a linear order, with words spoken one after another, even though the events represented may have happened simultaneously or in a different order from that in which they are spoken of. The grammatical structures have a behavioral impact, or role. For example, in the sentences 'The boy came home' and 'Johnny shot the tiger', both 'the boy' and 'Johnny' carry the grammatical role (function, meaning) of Actor. But this meaning, as a conditioned meaning variant, is (emically) extended to cover forms which may include some meaning differences which are not correlated with a grammatical form difference. In the sentence 'The tree fell', for example, 'the tree' is an emic actor conditioned by the referential inanimateness of a tree in contrast to the animate boy capable of volition. There is no grammatical form contrast in English correlated with the meaning difference, hence volitional difference at this point is contrastive only in the referential structure—not in the grammatical structure.

Referential structure is that to which the stream of speech refers, hence the characteristics of its sequence differ from those of the grammatical or telling sequence. There is simultaneity in the referential or happening order; many things may happen at once. Saint recorded the Waorani stories at the same time they were being told. Also the referential or happening sequence is fixed. Saint transcribed the stories before we made this study; that order is fixed, irreversable. Grammatical sequence, on the other hand, may be either essentially the same as, or quite different from the referential sequence, and admits little simultaneity except in special instances such as puns. In addition, the referential structure includes something of the view of the speakers of the language, such as purpose or explanation for events, the role a person or prop plays in those events, the talked-about beliefs, and truth values.

(2) The tagmeme is a UNIT-IN-CONTEXT. The grammatical unit-in-context is described in relation to four characteristics: (a) A tagmeme always occurs in a larger, including structure—i.e. in a slot in that structure. In general, through treatment of slot, emphasis is given to the nuclear versus marginal characteristic of the unit in relation to that larger context. (b) Class is the substance manifesting the unit. A set of several different classes may manifest a given tagmeme whereas the Slot-Role combination is unique to some one tagmeme. (c) Role identifies the function which the unit has in relation to other constituents of the immediately including

structure. (d) The fourth feature is cohesion in occurrence, as obligatory or optional to a governing structure; or it shows agreement with one or more characteristics of other tagmemes of its context. (Referential and phonological tagmemes are also characterized by slot, class, role, and cohesion; but the characteristics have different manifesting kinds of elements.)

Trees for Constituent Analysis from Discourse to Morpheme

Evelyn G. Pike

Every grammatical construction is made up of constituents. Each constituent is a unit-in-context. Units neither occur nor even exist in theory in isolation from action, thought, speech, or some kind of behavior which gives them their relevance, coherence with rationality, and emic content. Such a structure is inevitably hierarchical since man cannot handle vast detail unless it is reacted to as a complex of groupings of simple chunks as parts of larger chunks. Each chunk has a role to play in some place (slot) in a more inclusive element, but in turn is substitutable by some other chunk of a set (a class) in a way that the whole retains the same grammatical proportion of one part to another.

Here short texts are shown to be hierarchical by representing them as trees (upside down), with the story as a whole labelled at the top node (joining of branches). Branches downwards have a label above them identifying their general functional place in larger structures; labels below them specify their grammatical relevance (role). At branch ends class labels appear. If the nucleus of a construction occurs alone, the name of the class filling that nucleus is usually given, or added in parenthesis, rather than that of the class made up of the nucleus plus one or more margins. For instance, in the English sentence 'Boys eat a lot', we would say that the class NOUN fills the subject-as-actor rather than NOUN PHRASE.

1. **Constituent structure trees for 'The Origin of the Rainbow' story.** Here the constituent structure of this particular text is presented as a whole, in the form of a tree diagram. Such a diagram only gives a preliminary etic view, because generalization must await numerous such analyses before general patterns can be seen. This analysis is incomplete in detail of subclasses and identification of some slots, roles, and classes. We have made no attempt to state cohesive features. (When the latter have been found, they can be presented as a set of formulas in a four-celled display.

Such general, emic structuring for clause and verb is presented, in tentative form, in the following two articles.)

In a tree diagram, the first occurrence of a term is given in full form. Later occurrences are usually abbreviated.

In Figure 1, from two to five layers of structure of the rainbow story are developed. For a detailed discussion of the theory and technology involved, see Pike and Pike (1977, 1983).

2. A sample of constituent structure trees for 'The Jaguar and the Turtle' story. The Jaguar and the Turtle (JT) story is now presented, using the same style of tree diagram and symbols as above. In Figure 12, higher layers of structure are presented, somewhat as in Figure 1 for the Rainbow story. In Figure 13, a part of the setting (1–4) is carried down to the levels of sentence cluster or sentence. In Figure 14, one branch (the Exchange Cluster 5–15) of the Resolved section (5–31) is presented to the level of various exchanges (5–15), still lower for the second exchange (5–8).

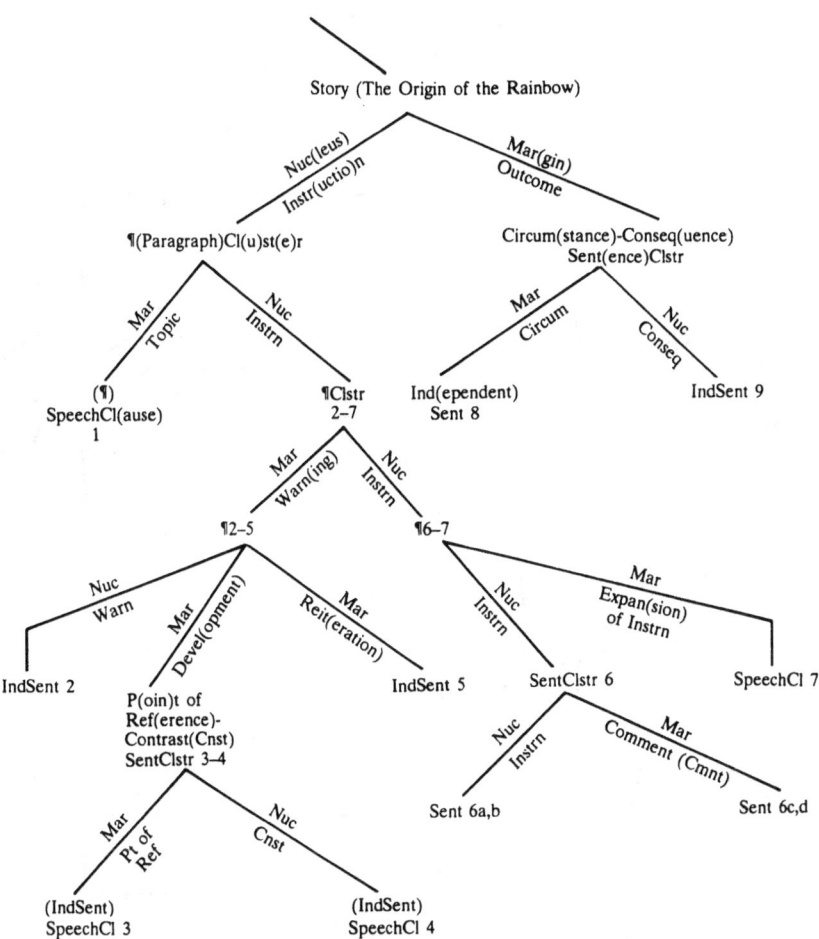

FIGURE 1. A Tree diagram for higher layers of grammatical structure of 'The Origin of the Rainbow', shown with slot (labelled above the branches), role (labelled below the branches), and class (labelled at the ends of the branches)

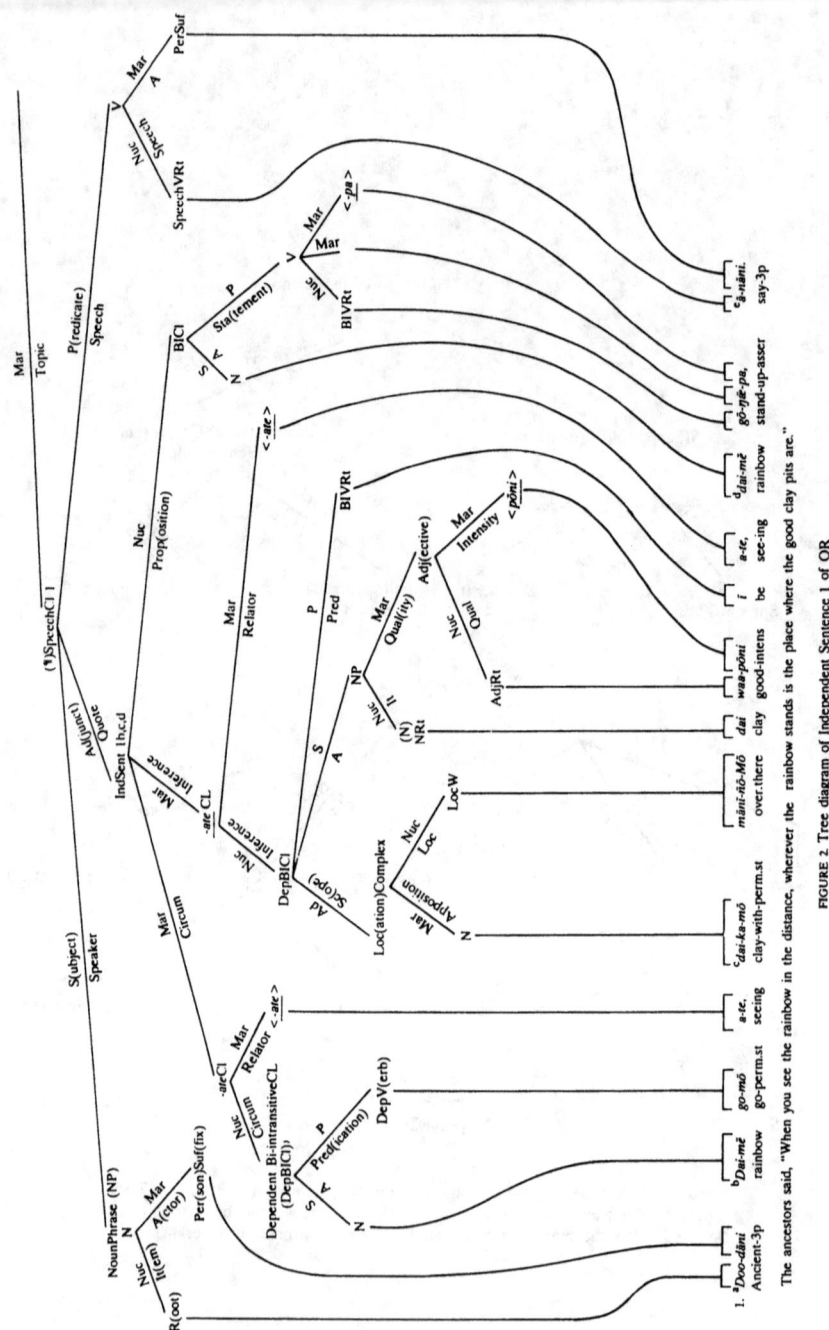

FIGURE 2 Tree diagram of Independent Sentence 1 of OR

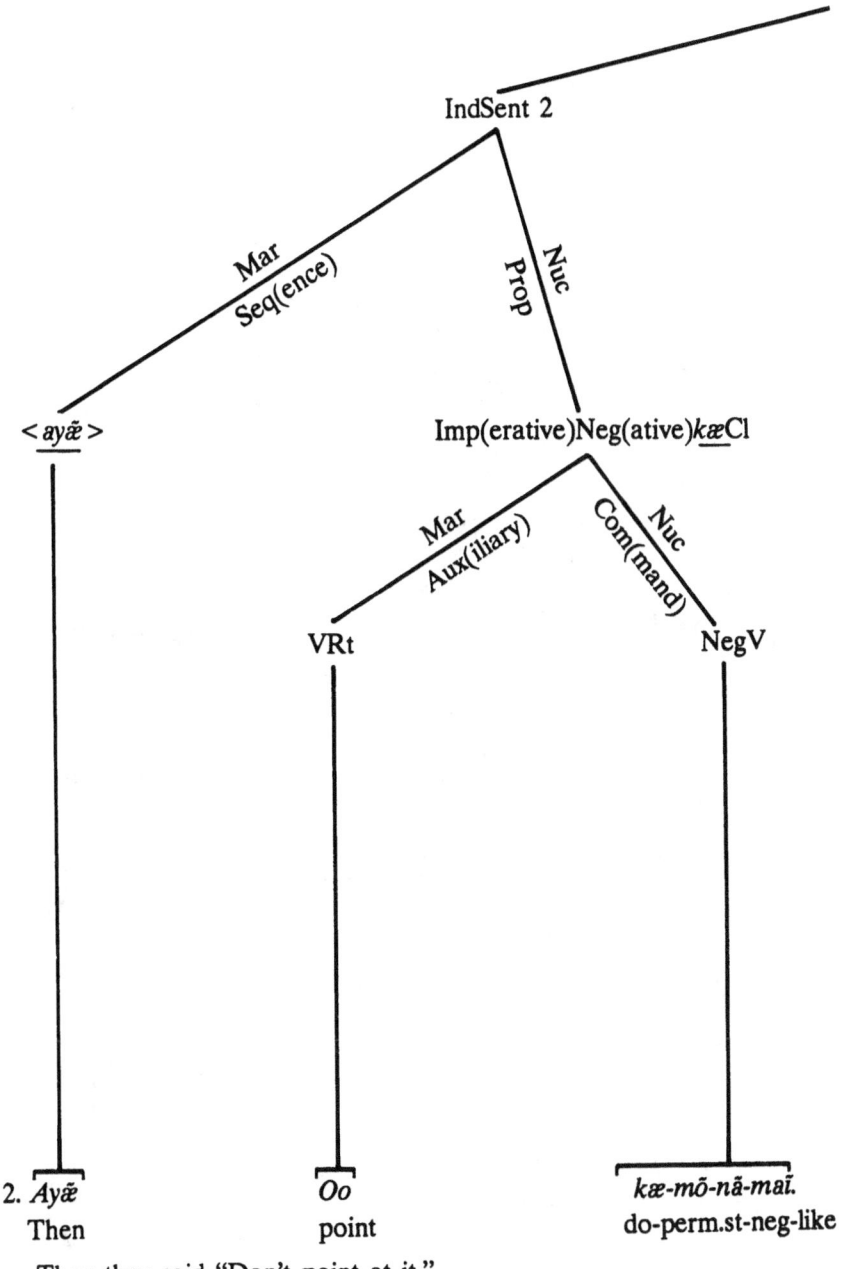

FIGURE 3. Tree diagram of Independent Sentence 2 of OR

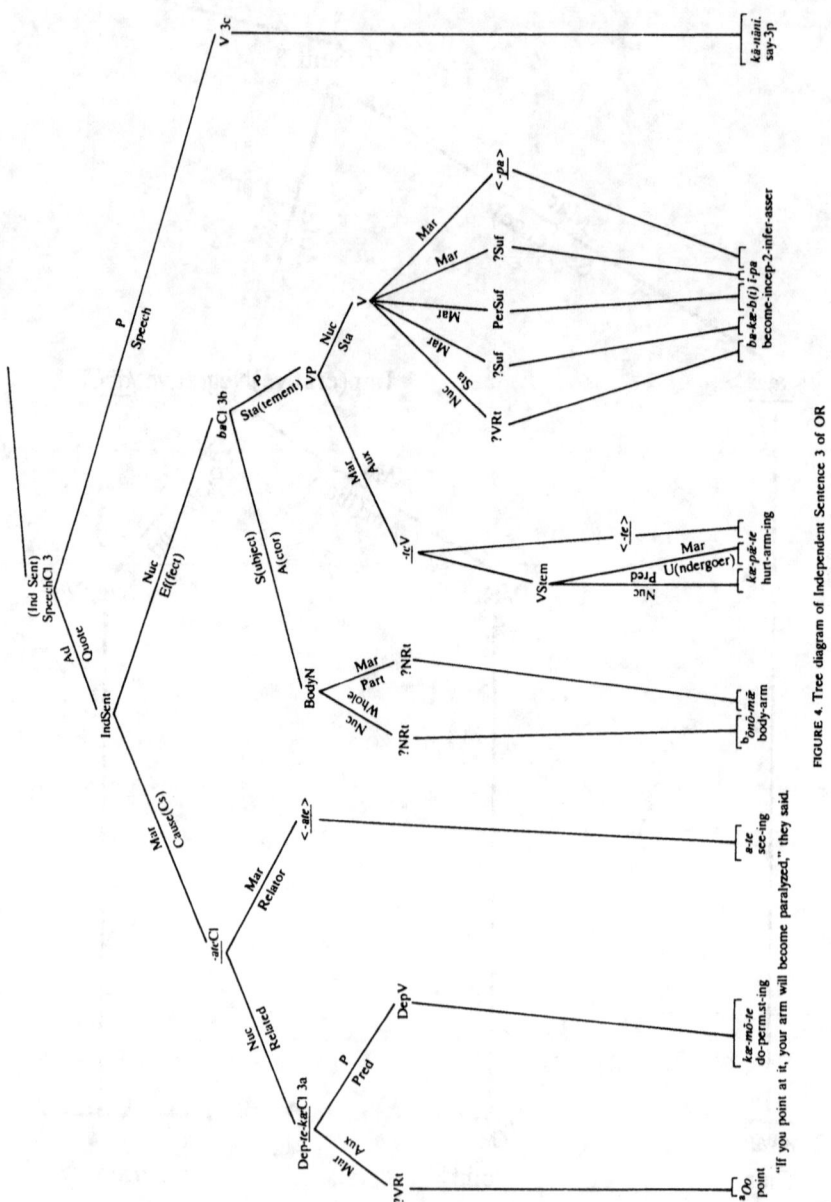

FIGURE 4. Tree diagram of Independent Sentence 3 of OR

Evelyn G. Pike: Trees for Constituent Analysis from Discourse to Morpheme 37

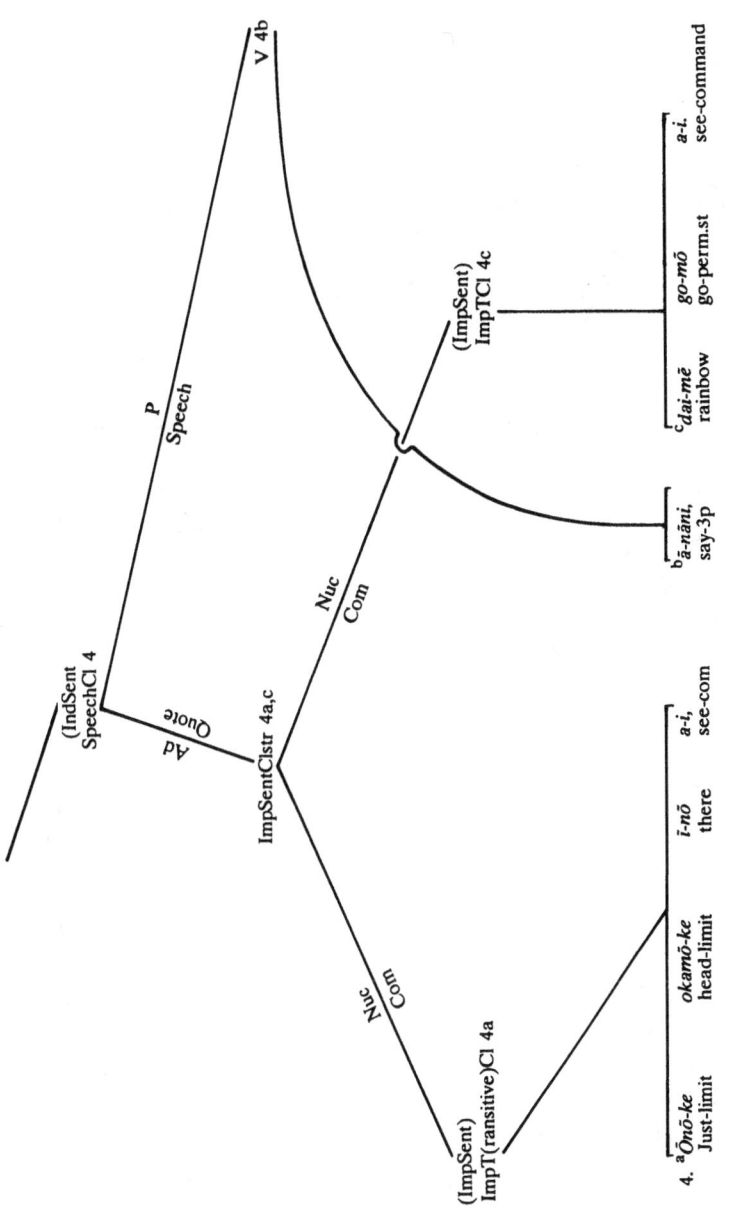

FIGURE 5. Tree diagram of Independent Sentence 4 of OR

"Just nod your head," they said, "Up there is the rainbow. Look over there."

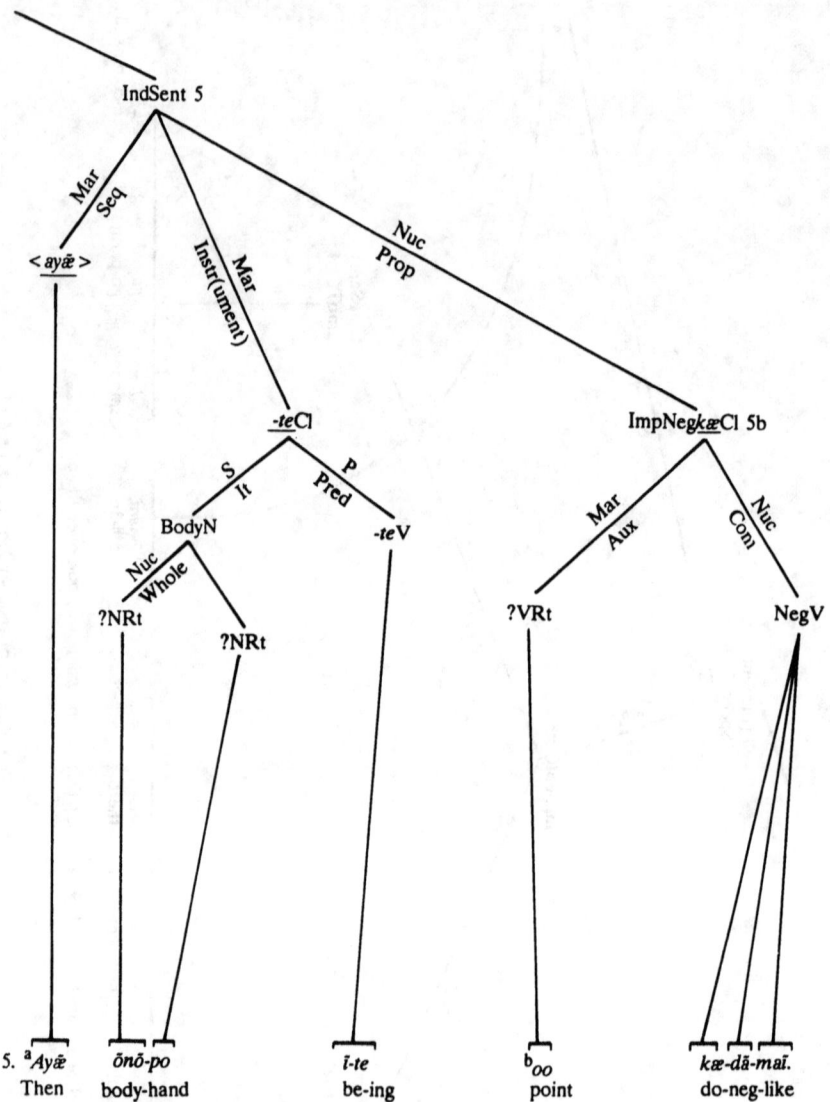

FIGURE 6. Tree diagram for Independent Sentence 5 of OR

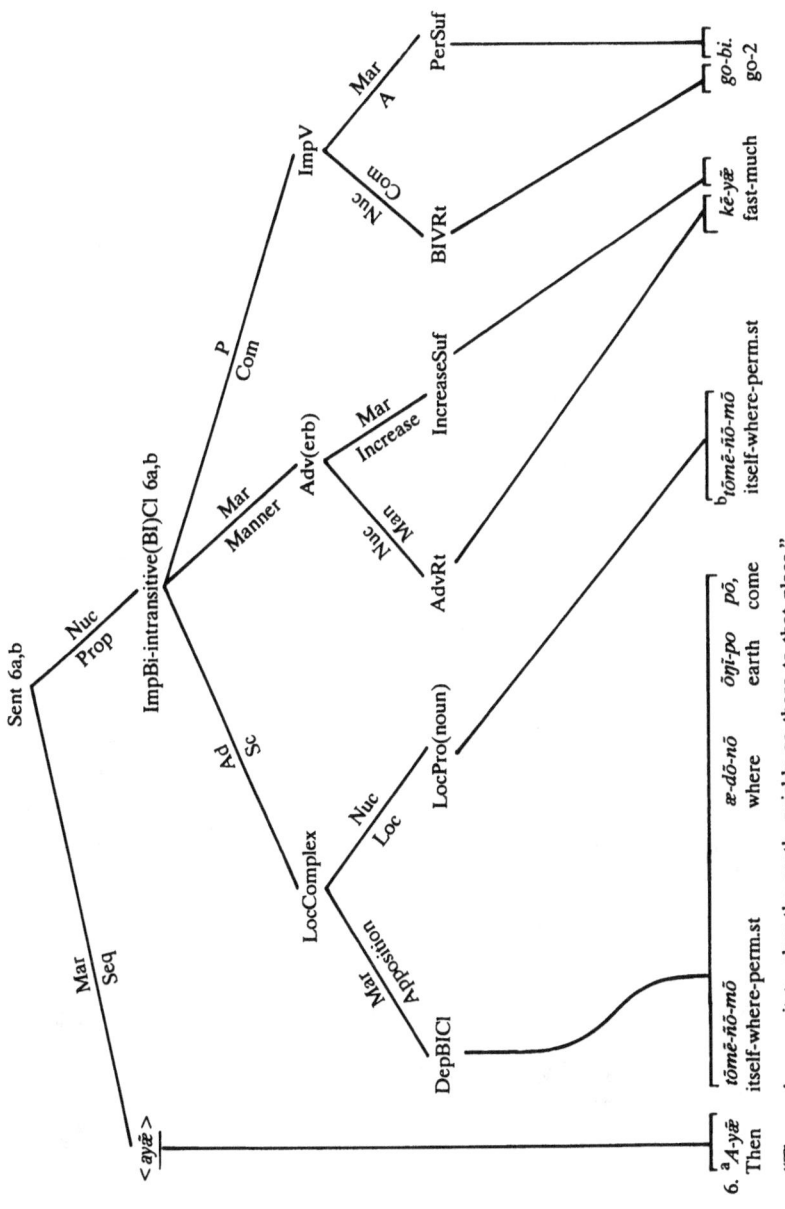

FIGURE 7. Tree diagram for Sentence 6a–b of OR

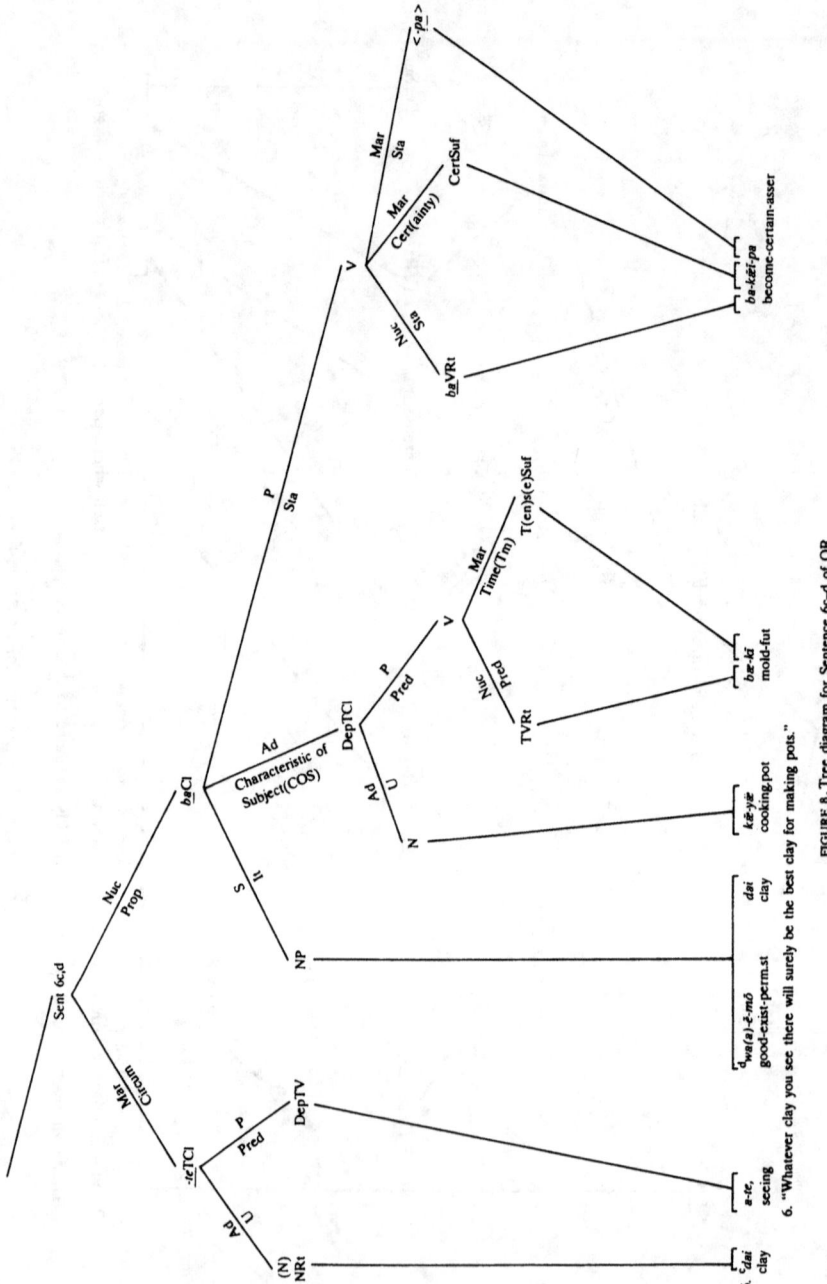

FIGURE 8. Tree diagram for Sentence 6c-d of OR

6. "Whatever clay you see there will surely be the best clay for making pots."

Evelyn G. Pike: Trees for Constituent Analysis from Discourse to Morpheme 41

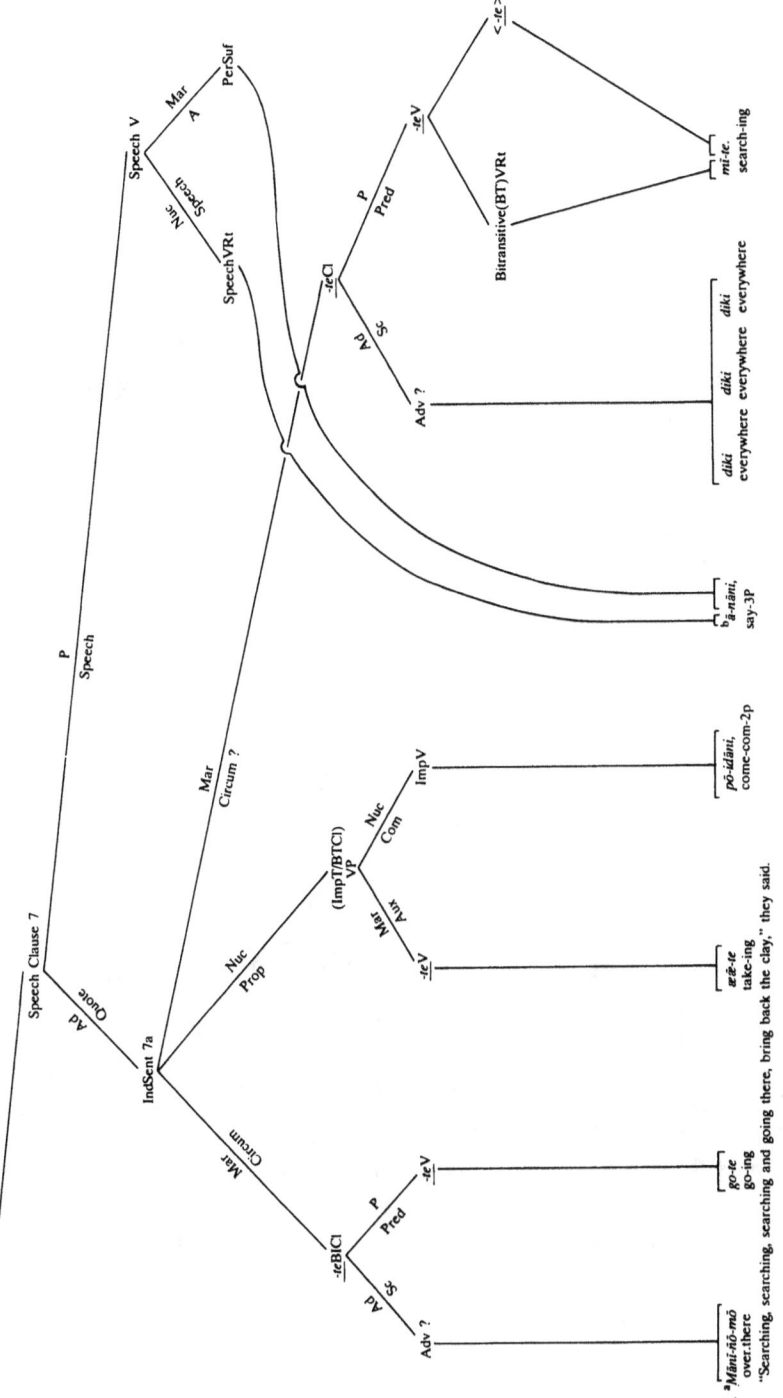

FIGURE 9. Tree diagram for Speech Clause 7 of OR

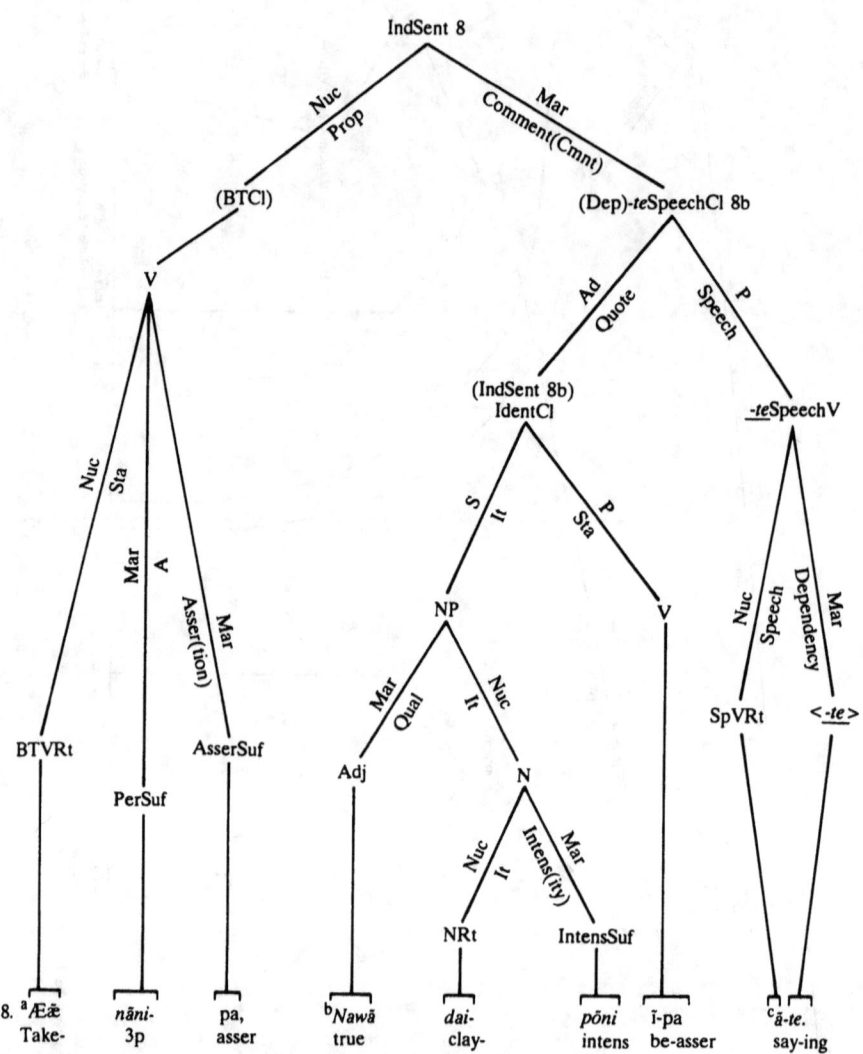

FIGURE 10. Tree diagram for Independent Sentence 8 of OR

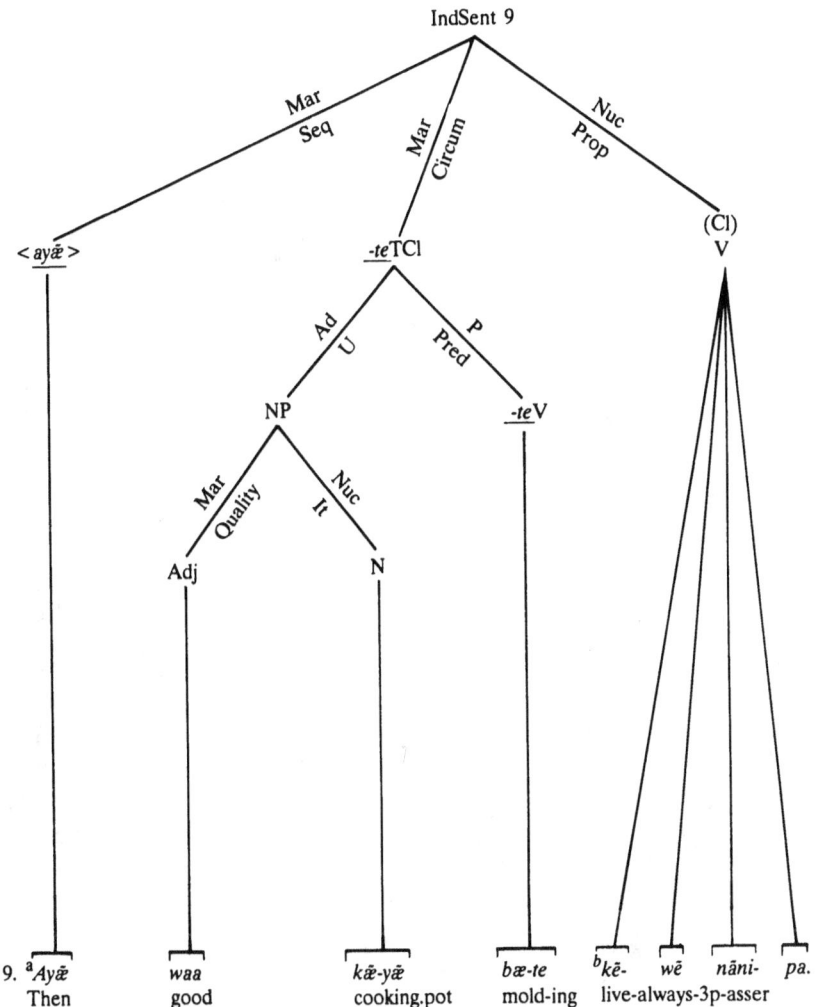

FIGURE 11. Tree diagram for Independent Sentence 9 of OR

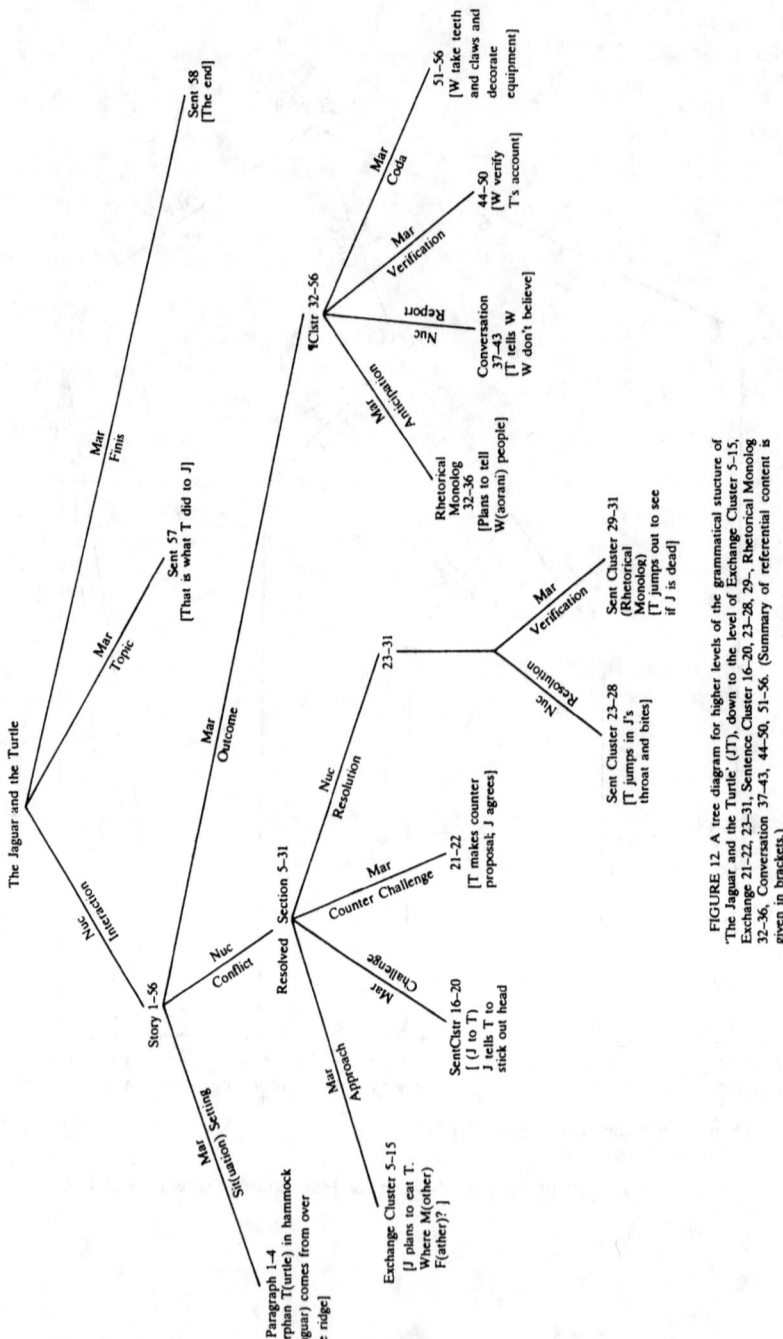

FIGURE 12. A tree diagram for higher levels of the grammatical structure of 'The Jaguar and the Turtle' (JT), down to the level of Exchange Cluster 5-15, Exchange 21-22, 23-31, Sentence Cluster 16-20, 23-28, 29-, Rhetorical Monolog 32-36, Conversation 37-43, 44-50, 51-56. (Summary of referential content is given in brackets.)

Evelyn G. Pike: Trees for Constituent Analysis from Discourse to Morpheme 45

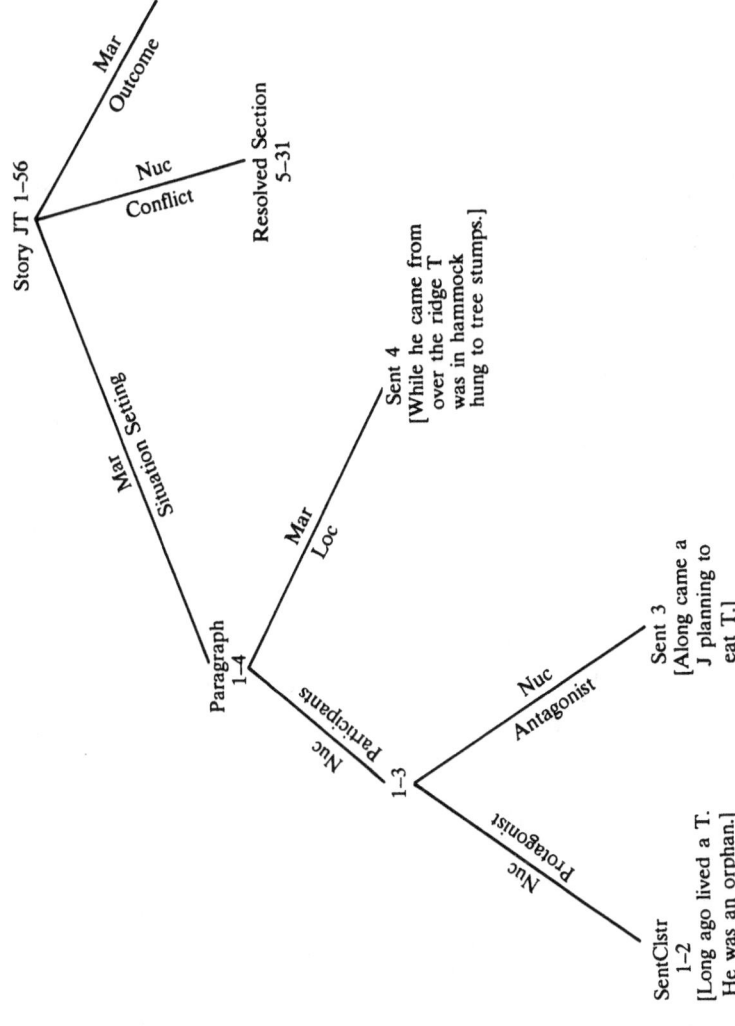

FIGURE 13. Tree diagram, from Margin as Setting of JT, down to level of Sentence 3,4 or Sentence Cluster 1-2

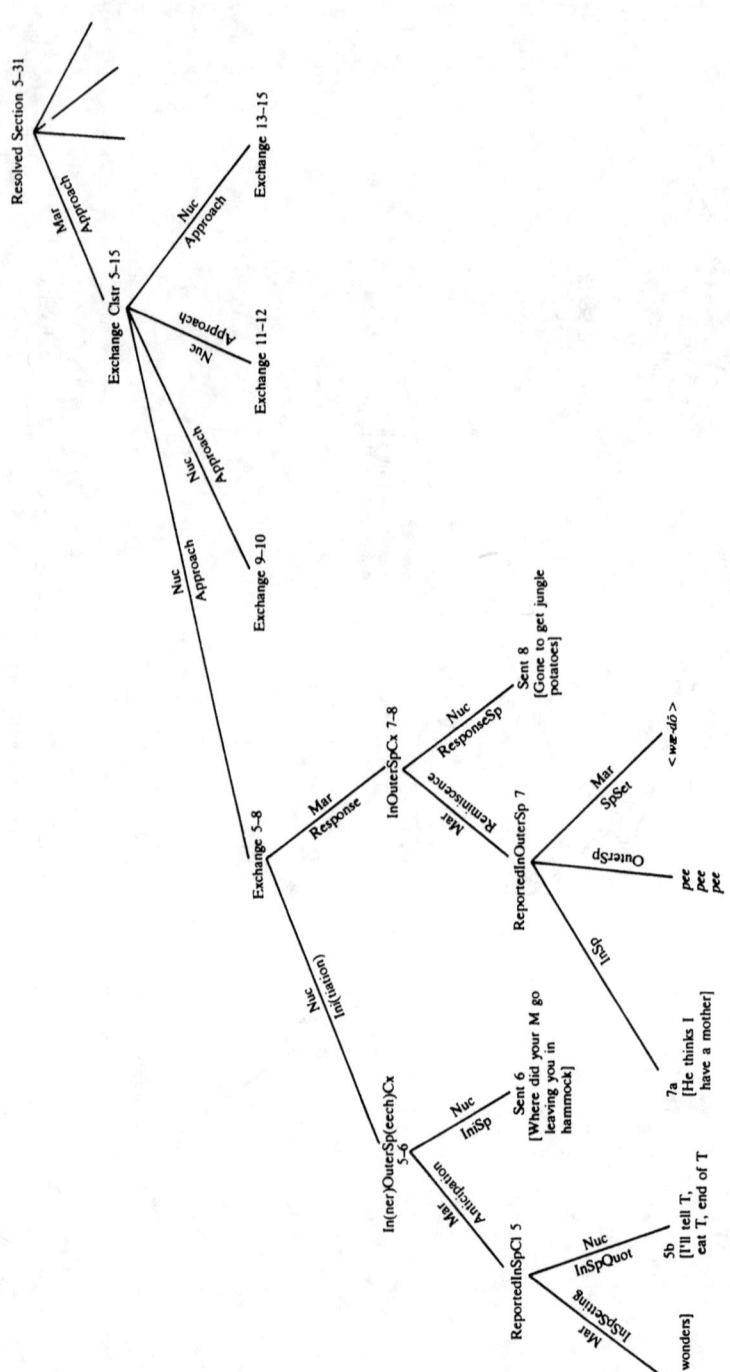

FIGURE 14. A tree diagram displaying grammatical constituents for the Exchange Cluster 5–15 down to Exchange level (5–8, 9–10, 11–12, 13–15), or (for 5–8) down to the various lower levels of quotation.

Waorani Clause Formulas

Patricia Wilkendorf

[A preliminary set of contrastive clause formulas shows the tagmemic sequences which comprise them. These formulas are intended to be emic, subject to revision, and filling gaps. The formulas show significant difference between major clause types, along with some options in content.]

Clauses differ grammatically by the kind and number of tagmemes which comprise them. Each tagmeme has slot (e.g. subject), class (e.g. noun phrase), role (e.g. actor), and cohesion (e.g. verb type controls or is controlled by the presence of undergoer, or both mutually control the permitted or required presence of the other). The following abbreviations are used.

Slot symbols: S (Subject), Mar (Margin), Co (Complement), Ad (Adjunct), P (Predicate).

Class symbols: NP (Noun Phrase), V (Verb), MW (Manner Word), LC (Location Complex), Aj (Adjective), TW (Time Word), VP (Verb Phrase), Dir (Directional Word), T (Time), Pn (Pronominal Word), Av (Adverb), Ger (Gerund), QW (Question Word).

Role symbols: It (Item), St (Statement), Sc (Scope), ! (Command), U (Undergoer), Q (Question), Inton (Intonation), ? (Interrogative), ChS (Character of Subject), Ac (Actor).

Cohesion symbols: x > (x controls), > x (controls x), > x > (x is controlled by one item and controls another, or mutually controlling), Id (Identity), BI (Biintransitive), Eq (Equational), / 'or'. A hypen [-] abbreviates the label of a slot-role combination such as S-Ac, which is to be read 'subject as actor'.

One or two illustrations of each clause type are given from the stories of the Origin of the Rainbow (OR), the Origin of Cassava (OC), or the Jaguar and the Turtle (JT); numbers represent the particular sentence. The Waorani material is given with the relevant word or phrase directly under the chart of the tagmeme which it manifests. In the initial stages of analysis, more extensive charts were made in this way with further illustrations from the texts to help establish the optional or obligatory occurrence of these tagmemes.

Following the illustrations, brief comments are given to prevent the reader from overlooking certain significant points, or to point out areas where the analysis is known to be incomplete.

1. Independent Identity Clause =

	S	NP	P	V
+	It	—	St	>Id>

OR 11 *Wao-bi   ī-mi-pa.*
       Waorani-2   be-2-asser
       You are an Waorani.

OR 12 *Wao-bi   i-mi-?*
       Waorani-2   be-2-?
       Are you a Waorani?

For Identity clauses, the verb is always *ī-* 'be'. As already shown by the formula, the interrogative word order is identical to that of the declarative, but the formulas differ slightly in that the interrogative clause ends in interrogative intonation. The Identity clause cannot be collapsed with the Equative clause for at least two reasons. Their interrogative formulas are different and the Identity clause only has S-It + P-St, whereas the Equative clause has S-It + Co-ChS + P-St. Their forms do not even appear identical when S-It is absent from the Equative clause, because in such cases Co-ChS is always an adjective or gerund, neither of which may occur as S-It of an Identity clause.

2. Independent Equative Clause =

Mar	MW	Mar	LC	S	NP	Co	Aj NP Ger	P	V
±		±		±		+		+	
Man	—	L	—	It	—	ChS	—	St	>Eq>

OC 7 *Mānō-maī   ōnō weka   kēwē   mǣ   ōñō.*
         that-like   river beside   cassava   flat   remain
    They are right there beside the river where cassava plants grow.

OR 22   *Dai-mē   ñǣnǣ   ī-pa.*
                                        rainbow   big   be-asser
        The rainbow is big.

The word *ayǣ* 'then, later' is normally a clause connector, but in OC 65a it appears to act as an adverb in the verb phrase. In JT 5d, there seems to be a reversal of the normal word order for an Equative clause (possibly because the jaguar wants to emphasize the fact that the turtle will be DEAD).

3. Independent Intransitive Clause =

Mar	LC	S	NP	Mar	TW	P	VP
±		±		±		+	
L	—	Ac	—	T	—	St	>I>

OC 39   *Doo-dāni   wēē-nē   kē-wē-ŋa-dān(i)-ī-pa.*
              old-3p   long.ago-in   live-always-far.pst-3p-infer-asser
        The ancestors lived long long ago.

Alternative Word Order: Mar-T P-St S-Ac

JT 1   *Wēē-nē   kē-wē-ŋā-ta-pa   titæke   ado-kā-ke*
           long.ago-in   live-always-3-pst-asser   turtle   one-3-limit
        Long long ago a turtle lived all alone.

The most interesting phenomenon occurring in the Declarative Intransitive clause is the change in word order for JT 1 and 16. The turtle, as Subject, is mentioned after the verb instead of before it. Due to the early occurrence of these two examples in the text, the shift could be to show the insignificance usually attributed to the turtle, which is contraindicated later in the story. To substantiate this claim, one needs only to refer to the transitive clauses JT 54b and 57 (at the very end of the text) where the Ad/U is found out of its normal word order, directly after the verb rather than directly before it. In both cases the jaguar or the jaguar's claws and teeth are involved and this is because it is now the jaguar who is insignificant, or at least powerless.

Finally, regarding Intransitive Clause formulas, in spite of the fact that both Location and Time appear in the formula as separate tagmemes, they never appear together in one clause.

4. Independent Biintransitive Clause =

	Mar/Mn	MW/—		S/Ac	NP/—		Mar/T	TW/—		Ad/S	N Dir/—		P/St	VP/>BI>
	±		±			±			±			+		

OR 21   *Dai-mē*   *ĩ-ñõ-mõ*   *gõ-ŋǣ-pa.*
         rainbow   here-where-perm.st   stand-up-asser
         The rainbow is there.

Alternative Word Order = S-Ac P-St Ad-Sc

OC 11b *titæ nāŋī nāŋī nāŋī kōwē kĕ-wē   kĕwē weka.*
       tapir lots lots lots always live-always cassava beside
       Lots and lots of tapirs lived right there beside the cassava patch.

A time expression appears only once in the data (OC 82) in this clause type, but it occurs in the same position as in the Intransitive clause examples, so that it is evidently not an irregular form or example.

In OC 11b, note the position of the Ad-Sc following the verb. It has not been possible to explain this, because the phrase *kĕwē weka* appears only once in the data.

5. Independent Transitive Clause =

Mar	MW	Mar	TW	Mar	L	S	Pn	Ad	Av NP
±		±		±		±		±	
Mn	—	T	—	L	—	Ac	—	U	—

JT 45   *Mānī-ñō-mō-nō*   Ñæ̃wæ̃næ̃
                          there-where-perm.st-twd.other   Ñæ̃wæ̃næ̃

	P	VP
+	St	>T>

     wāā̃   kæ-bo   wæ̃-ta-pa
     overcome do-1   die-pst-asser
     Right there where I conquered Ñæ̃wæ̃næ̃, the jaguar, and he died.

Alternative Word Order: Mar-Mn   S-Ac   P-St   Ad-U

JT 57 *Mānō-maī titæke kæ-kā-ta-pa mēñe.*
         that-like   turtle   do-3-pst-asser jaguar
         That's what the little turtle did to the big jaguar.

Problem areas in the declarative transitive clause formula include the fact that *kōwē* 'always' can appear before the Undergoer rather than with the verb, which puts an emphasis on what is receiving the action rather than on what the action itself is.

Ñōwo 'now' can occur after the subject rather than before, possibly for emphasis.

The word order for marginal modifiers is somewhat complicated by the presence of varieties (L, T, Mn), although no more than two appear at any one time. Manner appears before Time but does not occur in our data in an example with Location. Time and Location also do not appear together in one transitive clause.

One last major problem which needs to be dealt with is the problem of implied Undergoer; this will be treated in the concluding section of this paper.

6. Independent Bitransitive Clause =

Mar	MW	S	N Pn	Ad	Dir NP	Ad	N V Av	P	VP
± Mn	—	± Ac	—	± Sc	—	± U	—	+ St	>BI>

JT 12a   Badā   īnō   kōwǽ   ǽǽ-kæ go-dā
                 mother   over.there potato take-incep go-3h
Mother has gone a little way down the trail to get jungle potatoes.

In the Bitransitive clause formula worksheets, OC 38 and JT 35 show the concept of reciprocal verbs referred to by Peeke (1979:79) as the action of a subject and the reaction of the recipient appearing in the same clause. For example,

OC 38 *Mānō-maī Kadæ mōni-tō ī-mōni-tō apǽ-ne-kā   ēñē-ta-mōni-pa.*
        that-like   Kadæ 1p-pn be-1p-ing speak-mouth-3 hear-pst-1p-asser
That's the way Kadæ told us the story.

The possible grammatical classes filling in as Ad-U include nouns and verb forms.

In the Waorani language there are two ways to indicate a question, regardless of the clause type: either by using an interrogative word (normally at the beginning of the clause, as in 12 below or clause-medially as in 13a below) or by an intonational pattern on the verb which indicates that it is a question rather than a statement. The Interrogative Transitive clause seems always to occur with the Interrogative word following the subject (if the latter is present within the clause).

7. Independent Imperative Intransitive Clause =

P	VP
!	>I>

OC 36a *Pō   a-i-dāni*
       come see-command-2p
All of you, come and see!

Intransitive commands only require a verb in the formula (with no optional elements) and the bitransitive command requires Ad-Sc and a verb. Transitive commands have an optional Undergoer and a required verb, while bitransitive commands have both an optional Undergoer and Scope

Patricia Wilkendorf: Waorani Clause Formulas

and a required verb. In both of the transitive-type commands, the reciprocal verbs can appear (OC 25c, JT 17b, 19b).

8. Independent Imperative Biintransitive Clause =

$$\pm \frac{Ad \mid Dir}{Sc \mid -} + \frac{P \mid VP}{! \mid >BI>}$$

OR 4b ī-nõ   a-i
       there   see-command
       Look over there!

9. Independent Imperative Transitive Clause =

$$\pm \frac{Ad \mid NP}{U \mid -} + \frac{P \mid VP}{! \mid -}$$

OC 13 Bo-tõ   ī-mo-te æǣ–ŋī-m(i)-ī-pa.
       1-pn   be-1-ing take-fut-2-infer-asser
       Take me!

10. Independent Imperative Bitransitive Clause =

$$\pm \frac{Ad \mid NP}{U \mid -} \pm \frac{Ad \mid NP}{Sc \mid -} + \frac{P \mid \overset{LC}{VP}}{! \mid >BT>}$$

OC 14 Bo-tõ yæwa mãnī õŋīpo-dẽ ǣ wo-ga-bi.
       1-pn root there ground-in up pull-roll-2
       Pull up my root from the ground.

11. Independent Interrogative Transitive Clause =

$$\pm \frac{Ad \mid N}{U \mid -} + \frac{P \mid VP}{Q \mid -} + \frac{Mar \mid \text{'?'}}{? \mid -}$$

OR 17 Dai-mẽ   a-bi   ?
       rainbow   see-2   ?
       Do you see the rainbow?

53

While analyzing the clause structure of transitive verbs, it became very clear in the last two texts that the Waorani language does not require an explicit Undergoer within a transitive or bitransitive clause. This means that sometimes there is no noun phrase, noun, or pronoun to mark the undergoer. Adjunct as Undergoer is implied in transitive clauses in one of three other ways, as the following chart shows: (1) by prior explicit reference in preceding sentences of the text, (2) by implication of the verb root in the clause in question, and (3) by the use of noun identifiers as affixes in the verb. Illustrations of these follow.

Text Reference	Missing Ad-U	How Implied in Text
OC 1	story	implied by verb 'speak'
OC 21	cassava root	prior reference OC 20a
OC 22	cassava root	prior reference OC 20a
OC 29d	cassava root	prior reference OC 28a
OC 30e	cassava root	prior reference OC 28a
OC 43b	cassava root	prior reference OC 31b, 32b
OC 38	story	implied by verb 'speak'
JT 20b	head	implied in 'put out head id'
JT 21c	tongue	'put out tongue id-2'
JT 21d	head	'put out head id'
JT 25b	throat	'bite-esophagus id-3'
JT 36	it (event)	prior reference in JT 31, 32
JT 42	story	implied by verb 'say'
JT 43	jaguar	prior reference in JT 38b *Nǣwǣnǣ*
JT 51	jaguar	implied in JT 45a *Nǣwǣnǣ*
JT 55b	claws & teeth	prior reference JT 54b

12. Independent Interrogative Equative Clause =

Mar	QW	Co	Aj NP	P	VP
+ ?	—	+ ChS	—	+ Q	>Eq>

OC 10 Kĩ n(o)ã te   titæ nãŋĩ   ē-wa-ta-wo.
        why   tapir lots   exist-foot.id-pst-dubi
"I wonder why there are so many tapir tracks," he thought.

	S	N	Co	Aj NP Ger	P	VP	Mar	'?'
±	It	—	ChS	—	Q	—	?	—

OR 32 ōnō-mæ̃   kæ-pæ̃-te   ī-mi   ?
       body-arm.id hurt-arm.id-ing be-2   ?
       Does your arm hurt?

13. Independent Interrogative Intransitive Clause =

	S	Pn	Mar	QW	P	VP
±	Ac	—	?	—	Q	>I>

JT 6a Bi-tõ badã   ædōnō   go-dã
       2-pn mother   where   go-3h
       Where has your mother gone?

	S	Pn	P	VP	Mar	'?'
+	Ac	—	Q	—	Int	—

OC 54 Bi-tõ   go-dã-maī ī-mi   ?
       2-pn   go-neg-like be-2 ?
       Are you not going?

Waorani Verb Affixes

Thomas W. Holman

Waorani Verbs exhibit a great deal of variation in the occurrence of affixes. This paper presents preliminary findings concerning that variation. The underlying assumption is that some of this variation can be explained in terms of the function (role) which a verb has in an independent clause (Pike and Pike 1977:35–57). I have found, for example, that verbs which fill the nuclear (predicate) slot of an independent declarative clause tolerate more affixes than verbs which fill the nuclear slot of an independent imperative clause. In the former case, the role of the verb is statement whereas in the latter its role is command.

The analysis is based on the following Waorani texts: The Origin of the Rainbow (OR), The Origin of Cassava (OC), and The Origin of the Corn Bees (CB) by Dayuma; The Jaguar and the Turtle (JT), The Alligator and the Bird (AB), The Spider Monkey's Tail (TL), The Spider Monkey's Thumbs (TH), and The Tapir (TP) by Giketa; and Bluebird's Report (BR) by Wiña.

The presentation is organized into three major sections discussing the relationships among affixes for verbs in three types of independent clauses. Belatedly, a fourth type—the independent request clause—was identified. Its analysis has been included as an addendum to the section on verbs in imperative clauses. For each type of clause, two questions are answered: (1) How are the affixes ordered with respect to each other? In particular, how do they group into classes which fill the slot-roles of the verb? (2) What restrictions of occurrence exist between them? At the beginning of the discussion of each type, a tagmemic formula for the verb is given which graphically summarizes the affixal relationship for verbs in that particular slot-role.

The following criteria were used to identify the slot-role for independent verbs used in this analysis. It allowed approximately 40% of all verbs in the text materials to be identified.

(1) All verbs ending with *pa* 'assertive' mark independent clauses.

(2) All verbs with *i* 'command' and *bã-we (mã-we)* 'urgent command-remonstrative' mark independent imperative clauses. Sometimes *dã-maĩ (nã-maĩ)* 'negative-like' also marks imperatives, as in OR 5.

(3) Interrogative clauses are marked either by an interrogative word in the clause or by interrogative intonation. The interrogative words are *kĩ-nõ-ã-te* 'why', *kĩ-nõ* 'what', *æ-dõ-nõ* 'where', *æ-dõ* 'when', *æ-dõ-mẽ* 'where-speculative', and *æ-bã-nõ* 'how, what'.

(4) Where none of the above apply, sometimes the context and the free translation make it reasonably clear what slot-role a verb fills. For example, the verb *põ-ŋã* 'come-3' in the following example is an independent declarative verb, judging from its position in the sentence and the free translation.

OC 8   *Kĩ-nõ ĩ   ã-n(ẽ)-ĩ-ke   wa-dæ põ-ŋã*
         what be say-perf-infer-limit away come-3
         Still wondering about it, the Waorani left.

Verbs in declarative, interrogative, and imperative independent clauses were examined. The roles of the verbs occurring in these clauses are statement, question, and command, respectively. In addition, the role of request for permission has been posited for verbs in the independent request clause.

1. Verbs in declarative clauses.

Verbs in the role of statement in the declarative clause show the widest variation in affixes. The tagmemic formula for the verb which fills the nuclear slot in the role of statement in the independent declarative clause is presented below. These findings provide a point of contrast for the discussion of the interrogative and imperative clauses which follow.

Independent Declarative Verb =

Nuc	V Root V Stem hc	Mar	dẽ (nẽ) 'perf' kæ 'incep'
±		±	
Pred	—	Asp	—

Mar	ta 'past' ga (ŋa) 'far past' kī (ŋī) 'future'	Mar	Per
±		±	
T	1.	Ac	—

Mar	kǽī 'certain' dẽ-ī 'perf-infer' te-ī 'ing-infer' ī 'inferential'	Mar	pa 'asser'
±		±	
Infer	1.	Mode	1.

An alternate order: Actor before Time when second or third person and past tense *(ta)* both occur.

Restrictions of occurrence:

1. Presence of *pa* 'assertive' with *ga* 'far past' requires either *ī* 'inference' or *te-ī* 'resultative'; and *pa* with *kī (ŋī)* 'future' requires *ī* 'inference'.

2. If *kǽī* occurs, tagmemes of Aspect, Time, or Actor do not occur.

1.1. Order of affixes. This section attempts to identify the order of affixes in terms of their roles within a verb in a declarative clause. A computer program called Paradigm was utilized to assist in this phase of analysis. The program was developed by J. A. Bickford while a student at the Summer Institute of Linguistics program of the University of Texas at Arlington and is based on an earlier program written by Grimes and procedures devised by Grimes and others (Grimes 1967, 1978, 1979).

Five roles are posited, which normally occur in the order aspect, time, actor, inference, and mode, respectively. Some variation in the order of time and actor, as mentioned above, is predictable.

Affixes which fill the role of aspect generally indicate the shape of an event. For verbs in declarative clauses, these affixes are *kæ* 'inceptive', and *dẽ (nẽ)* 'perfective'. The suffix *kæ* generally indicates that an action is about to begin.

TP 57 *Wæ̃po wæ̃-kæ-kā-ī-pa*
father die-incep-3-infer-asser
Your father is about to die.

The suffix *dē (nē)* 'perfective' generally indicates that an event is completed.

TL 19 *Deye ōnō-no wa-dānī ī-nāni wĕmōka bedō-nē æmæ̃wo.*
monkey river-out other-3p be-3p secretly drown-perf last.time
Never again did the spider monkeys grab and drown others at the river.

The tense suffixes fill the role of time. They are *ta* 'past', *ga (ŋa)* 'far past', and *ki (ŋī)* 'future'. The ordering of *kæ* 'inceptive' and *ta* 'past' in the following example suggests that aspect suffixes precede tense suffixes.

JT 49 *Babæ ā-pa babæ ā-pa ā ī-kæ-ta-mō-pa.*
wild say-asser wild say-asser say be-incep-pst-1p-excl-asser
We kept saying, "You are talking wild. You are talking wild."

Person-gender-number suffixes (from now on referred to as person suffixes) fill the role of actor. In some instances, the person suffix precedes the tense suffix; in others, it follows the tense suffix. However, this variation is predictable. Second- and third-person suffixes precede the past-tense suffix *ta*. Otherwise, the person suffixes follow the tense suffixes (Peeke 1973:120).

The following examples illustrate this ordering, first with the suffix *dāni (nāni)* '3p' and then with *kā (ŋā)* '3'.

OC 37 *æ̃æ̃-nāni-ta-pa*
take-3p-pst-asser
they took

JT 37 *go-kā-ta-pa*
go-3-pst-asser
he went

OC 1 *apæ̃-ne-ga-dāni-ī-pa*
speak-mouth-far.past-3p-infer-asser
they spoke long long ago

OC 17 *go-dē-ŋa-kā-ī-pa*
go-perf-far.past-3-infer-asser
it spilled and spread out all over the place

While there were no occurrences of *ga (ŋa)* with the second-person suffixes in the texts, the following example of mi '2' and ta 'past' suggests that they have the same order as third-person suffixes.

BR 25 ã-mi-ta-?
    say-2-pst-?
    did you say . . . ?

As implied above, the first-person suffixes follow the tense suffixes. The following examples show this with *ta* 'past', *kĩ (ŋĩ)* 'future', and *bo (mo)* 'first-person singular'.

OC 36 æ̃æ̃-ta-bo-pa
    take-pst-1-asser
    I took (the tapir's cassava)

BR 1 apæ̃-ne-kĩ-ĩ-mo-?
    speak-mouth.id-fut-infer-1-?
    Shall I speak?

(The preceding verbs from BR 25 and BR 1 occur in independent interrogative clauses.)

The suffix *ĩ* 'inference' fills the role of inference. Peeke (1973:51) says that it marks a lack of authentication because the speaker did not (or does not yet) observe the action. This is the case when something is reported to have been said by the ancestors.

OC 1 Wẽẽ-nẽ   doo-dãni apæ̃-ne-ga-dãn(i)-ĩ-pa.
    long.ago-in ancient-3p speak-mouth.id-far.past-3p-infer-asser
    Long long ago the ancestors told this story.

Another suffix which also fills this role is *kæ̃ĩ (ŋæ̃ĩ)* 'certain'. The speaker refers to an event which he has not yet observed but which he feels certain will take place. The following example is typical of the use of *kæ̃ĩ*.

BR 25 nãnogæ̃ wæ̃-ŋæ̃ĩ-pa
    wife   die-certain-asser
    His wife will surely die.

The suffix *pa* 'assertive' fills the role of mode. It indicates the speaker's attitude toward an action or event and typically marks declarative clauses like OC 1 which is cited above.

1.2. Verb stems. The nuclear slot of a verb is filled by either a verb root or a verb stem. A verb stem is composed of a verb root plus a verb root or a verb root plus a verb-modifying morpheme, or a verb root plus a noun-classifier, as Peeke (1973:38) calls it. A simple verb root is illustrated in the following example.

JT 3 *mēñe pō-ŋā*
    jaguar come-3
    A jaguar was coming.

A stem based on two verb roots is illustrated in the following example. *Wo* 'float' and *ga* 'roll' together mean 'dig up'.

OC 28 *Ayæ kā-nā   wo-ga-kī-mi-ī-pa*
    then cassava.root pull-roll-fut-2-infer-asser
    Then dig up the cassava root.

In the next example, verb root plus modifying morpheme, the negative morpheme *wī* 'not' combines with *mō* 'sleep' to form a verb stem meaning 'dream'.

TP 14 *Titae-baī tǣnō-te wī-mō-ta-bo-pa.*
    tapir-like spear-ing not-sleep-pst-1-asser
    I dreamed that I speared a tapir.

Also, the verb stem *a-baī* 'see-like' communicates the concept 'get an idea', as in JT 21.

JT 21 *a-baī-pa*
    see-like-asser
    had an idea

The verb modifying morpheme may also indicate the direction of the action like *ŋ-* 'up' in OR 1.

OR 1 *daī-mē gō-ŋā-pa*
    rainbow stand-up-asser
    wherever the rainbow stands

In 2c, concerning noun-classifiers within the verb stem, Peeke (1973:38) says that they "function as incorporated object" in the verb construction. For example, *mi-* 'tail' is the object of *taa* 'cut' in TL 9.

TL 9 *bo-tõ taa-miæ̃-kæ-bo-ĩ-pa*
       1-pn   cut-tail.id-incep-1-infer-asser
       I'm going to cut off his tail.

A noun-classifier also may qualify a stative verb, as *po* 'finger identifier' does for *ẽ* 'exist' in TH 1.

TH 1 *Deye   ĩ-maĩ   wẽẽ-nẽ   ẽ-po-kã-ta-pa.*
       Spider.monkey this-like long.ago-in exist-finger-3-pst-asser
       Long ago the spider monkey had four fingers and a thumb.

In these two examples, however, the roles of the noun classifiers differ. In the former the role is embedded object or undergoer, and in the latter the role is embedded specifier or characteristic of subject. To posit a single separate slot-role on an affix level for the noun-classifiers in the verb construction, on a par with those mentioned in section 1.1, for aspect, time, person, and mode would obscure these role differences. For this reason, including them as part of a verb stem is preferred. Different types of verb stems could then be posited, such as transitive verb stem and stative verb stem for the above examples. This would allow the contrast in functions of noun-classifiers to be preserved.

1.3. Complex affixes. Complex affixes are pairs of affixes which fill single marginal slots of the verb. Five complex affixes which occur in the declarative clause verb are (1) *kæ-dõ* 'inceptive-contingent pst (conjectural)', (2) *kæ-ta* 'inceptive-pst (habitual pst)', (3) *kæ̃ĩ (ŋæ̃ĩ)* 'certain', (4) *te-ĩ* 'ing-inferential', and (5) *nẽ-ĩ (dẽ-ĩ)* 'perfective-inferential'. The first two have the role of time, and the last three have the role of inference (Wise 1963).

The complex affix *kæ-dõ* functions as Time in that it shifts the event spoken of into hypothetical time. In The Tapir story, for example, Giketa reports that Kenta speared a black panther. But in TH 8, he hypothesizes that if Kenta and Awæ̃ñetæ̃ had gone together to hunt, Awæ̃ñetæ̃ might have speared the black panther.

TP 8 *Gea   næ æ̃-te   gotebaĩ   Awæ̃ñetæ̃ waa*
       together carrying goinglike Aw-ñet   maybe

       tæ̃no-kæ-dõ-nẽ-ĩ-pa.
       spear-incep-twd.other-perf-infer-asser
       If they had gone together carrying their weapons, perhaps Awæ̃ñetæ̃ would have speared the black panther.

The complex affix *kæ-ta*, on the other hand, functions as time by indicating that a past event occurred habitually or repetitively. For example, in The Jaguar and the Turtle story, the Waorani admit that they were 'talking wild' when they used to accuse the turtle of 'talking wild'. The following could also be translated as 'we kept on saying'.

JT 49 ã ĩ-kæ-ta-mõ-pa
       say be-incep-pst-1p-excl-asser
       We used to say.

Peeke (1973:51) identifies the complex affix *te-ĩ* 'ing-inferential' as 'resultative'. This may indicate that a condition-result relationship is inferred between one event or state-of-being and a prior or subsequent event or state-of-being. The lack of cassava plants long ago, for example, is the condition which results in cassava becoming food for the Waorani.

OC 2 Wẽẽ-nẽ   kẽwẽ   dae ã-ŋa-te-ĩ-pa
      long.ago-in cassava none say-far.past-ing-infer-asser
      Long ago they had no cassava plants.

1.4. Restrictions of occurrence. One significant restriction of occurrence can be observed between tense, inferential, and mode suffixes. The presence of *pa* 'assertive' and either *ga (ŋa)* 'far past', *ki* 'future', or *kæ-dõ* 'inceptive-toward another (conjectural)' requires the presence of an inferential suffix. Since the presence of an inference marker implies that the speaker did not see the action, this relationship seems reasonable. One would not expect a speaker to be able to verify an event which happened long ago (far past), or which has yet to happen (future), or which is hypothetical (conjectural).

2. Verbs in interrogative clauses

As stated earlier, the underlying assumption of this analysis is that some of the difference in verb affixes can be explained in terms of the slot-role which a verb fills in a clause. In the independent interrogative clause, the verb fills the nuclear slot in the role of question. The suffixes and restrictions on occurrence which are unique to these verbs are discussed in this section.

Independent Interrogative Verb =

Nuc	V Stem V Root	Mar	ta 'past' ga (ŋa) 'far past' kī (ŋī) 'future'	Mar	Per
+		±		±	
Pred	—	T	1., 2., 3.	Ac	—

Mar	ī 'infer'	Mar	'V 'emphasis' wo 'dubitive' pa 'assertive'
±		±	
Infer	1.	Mode	1., 2., 3.

A does not precede T when second or third person and past tense *(ta)* occur together.

Restrictions of occurrence:

1. *pa* 'assertive' only occurs when *ga (ŋa)* 'far past' and *ī* 'inferential' occur together.
2. *wo* 'dubitative' only occurs with *ta* 'past'.
3. *'v* 'emphatic' only occurs with *kī (ŋī)* 'future' or no tense marker.

2.1. Order of affixes. While distribution of affixes is more limited for the interrogative verb, the order in which the affixes occur is the same as that for the declarative verb. For example, the variant ordering of the third-person and past-tense suffixes is found in AB 11 where *kā* 'third-person singular' occurs before *ta* 'past'.

AB 11 *æ-bā-nõ biwii kae-kā-ta-wo*
 how bird do-3-pst-dubitive
 I wonder how the little bird is doing?

Two mode suffixes are unique to the interrogative verb. They are *wo* 'dubitative' and *'V* (vowel) 'emphasis'. The suffix *wo* is generally used for mild questions, such as when the Waorani wonder about the little bird in AB 11 (cited above). The vowel suffix indicates a more intense question, such as when the jaguar interrogates the turtle about his mother.

JT 11 *Bi-tō badā nawāŋa bi-tō badā æ-dõ go-dā-'ā*
 2-pn mother truly 2-pn mother where go-3h-infer-emphatic
 Now tell me the truth little turtle. Where has your mother gone?

2.2. Restrictions of occurrence. It is difficult to determine when the restrictions of occurrence in our limited data are structurally significant and when they are simply due to lack of data. Two restrictions are noted here although their significance is uncertain. First, inferential suffixes occur only with the mode suffix *pa* 'assertive' in interrogative verbs. No inferential suffixes occur with either of the other two mode suffixes *wo* and *'V*.

JT 15 Badã æ-dõ-mẽ   go-ga-dã-ĩ-pa
       mother where-specula go-far.past-3h-infer-asser
       Mother! Where in the world did my mother go long, long ago?

Secondly, only certain tense and mode suffixes appear together. They are (1) *ga* 'far past' with *pa* 'assertive', (2) *ta* 'past' with *wo* 'dubitive', and (3) *kĩ (ŋĩ)* 'future' with *'V* 'emphasis'. The first two pairs are illustrated by JT 15 and AB 11, respectively (both cited above); the third is illustrated by TP 10.

TP 10 Titæ bo-tõ apæ-ne-kĩ-'ĩ-?
       tapir 1-pn speak-mouth.id-fut-emph-?
       Shall I tell you about the tapir?

3. Verbs in imperative clauses

Verbs which fill the nuclear slot of an independent imperative clause have the role of command. There is some variation in the order of affixes and in their restrictions of occurrence which are unique to these verbs.

Independent Imperative Verb =

	V Stem		dã-maĩ (nã-maĩ) 'neg-like'
	V Root	Mar	bã-we (mã-we) 'urgent com-remon'
Nuc			*i* 'command'
+---	---------	-----	---
Pred	—	Mode	1.

	dãni (nãni) '2p'
	da '2d'
Mar	bi (mi) '2'
±---	------------------
Ac	1.

Restrictions of occurrence:

1. Person suffixes only occur with the mode suffix *i* 'command', or *bã-we (mã-we)* 'urgent.command-remonstrative'.

3.1. Order of affixes. In contrast to both the declarative and interrogative verbs, two observations can be made regarding the order of affixes in imperative verbs. First, only person and mode suffixes occur. There is no evidence of aspect, tense, or inference markers in these verbs. Considering the nature of imperatives, this is not surprising. For example, imperatives are not expressed in either past or future tense. Secondly, the person suffixes follow the mode suffix, whereas they precede the mode suffix in other independent-clause verbs. In the following example, the person suffix *dāni (nāni)* '2d' follows the mode suffix 'command'.

BR 21 *wææ̃-i-dāni*
       down-command-2p
       You all come down!

A clarification of the suffixes *dāni (nāni)* and *da (na)* is in order here. In the declarative and interrogative verbs, *dāni* and *da* designate third person plural and third person dual, respectively. In imperative and request verbs, however, the same suffixes designate second person plural and dual, respectively. In these instances the person suffixes occur with (and follow) a mode suffix–either *i* 'command' or *bā-we* 'urgent command-remonstrative' for the imperative; or *e* 'permission' for the request verb (section **3.3**).

The role of mode is filled by *dā-maī (nā-maī)* 'negative-like', *i* 'command', and *bā-we (mā-we)* 'urgent command-remonstrative'. Their differences may be in degree of urgency as illustrated by BR 24 (above) and the following examples.

OC 26 *ææ̃-nā-maī*
      take-neg-like
      Don't take me yet.

TP 37 *Kæ̃-mæ̃, bado   kēyæ̃-mōni kæ-bā-we*
      Kæ̃mæ̃   pay.attention fast-intens   do-urgent.com-remon
      Kæ̃mæ̃, hurry. Come quick!

3.2. Restrictions of occurrence. One restriction is easily observed. Only second person suffixes take the role of actor. These include *dāni (nāni)* '2p', *da* '2d', and *bi (mi)* '2'. As with the limitation on tense suffixes, one would expect this limitation of person suffixes for imperatives.

Independent Request Verb =

```
       |        |     | bo (mo) '1'    |     |
       |        |     | mõ '1p excl'   |     |
  Nuc  | V Root | Mar | kã (ŋã) '3'    | Mar | e 'permission'
+ ─────┼────────┼─────┼────────────────┼─────┼─────────────────
  Pred |   —    | Ac  |       —        |Mode |        —

       |        | dãni (nãni) '2p'
   Mar |        | da (na) '2d'
± ─────┼────────┼──────────────────
  Granter of    |        —
  permission    |
```

3.3. Verbs in request clauses. The request clause was belatedly identified as a fourth type of indpendent clause. Verbs which fill the nuclear slot of this clause have the role of request for permission.

The imperative verbs and the request verbs are similar in that their mode suffixes occur in the medial position. This is in contrast with both declarative and interrogative verbs, where the mode suffix occurs in the final position.

In contrast with imperative verbs, request verbs have two person-suffix slots. The first of these names the actor role. The fillers for this slot are limited to first-person suffixes. They immediately follow the verb root and identify the actor of the action named by that verb root. The second slot names the granter-of-permission role and is filled only by second-person suffixes. It identifies the person of whom the request is made.

Another contrast with the imperative verb is that the actor suffix for the request verb precedes the mode suffix. In the imperative verb, the actor suffix follows the mode suffix. In the following example, Giketa requests of his two hunting companions that they let him spear a tapir.

TP 56 Õŋõ-i-da,   gīta-idi   yao   õŋõ-i-da   õ-ŋõ-mīna-te
       hold-com-2d   dog-plural grab   hold-command-2d   hold-2p-ing

        titæ-ke   ba-yõ   tǣnõ-mo-e-da   ã   a-pa.
        tapir-limit become-when   spear-1-permission-2d say see-asser

I said, "You two grab the dogs; let me spear that tapir by itself."

One occurrence restriction sets the request verb apart from the imperative verb: a person-as-actor suffix is required in every instance of the verb.

Conclusion

I have discussed in this paper some preliminary findings about the system of verb affixes in terms of the different roles a verb may have in an independent clause and the role and position of the affix internal to the verb and the verb stem. In the role of statement in a declarative clause, the verb tolerates five classes of affixes which have the roles of aspect, time, actor, inference, and mode. In the role of question in an interrogative clause, the verb has only four roles for its affixes—time, actor, inference, and mode. In contrast to the declarative verb, a different set of affixes fills the role of mode. In the role of command in an imperative clause, the verb has only the roles of actor and command mode for its affixes. In contrast to both the declarative and interrogative verbs, mode precedes actor. In the role of permission in a request clause, the verb, in addition to the roles of actor and mode, has a second affix for granter of permission. In contrast to the imperative clause, actor precedes the mode, and granter of permission follows the mode affix. Thus, in the Waorani language there is a correlation between the slot-role which a verb fills in an independent clause and the restrictions of occurrence of its affixes.

Part III

Some Referential Structures of Discourse

Some Referential Structures of Discourse

The world as we perceive it is structured. It is not experienced as molecules, atoms, or bits moving randomly. Similarly, the worlds of fiction or fantasy which we imagine are also structured. And the unseen elements which we deduce as present in any of these worlds are in their turn deduced as being structured.

To these worlds or elements of worlds our perception adds its contribution. To relations in our social world, we add judgments as to the purpose or role of the cast of actors in it. To our view of the background situations in which these characters act, we add our perceptions of their relevance, utility, or intended purpose in relation to our own experience or values or to those reported about our contemporaries or predecessors. And to the backdrop of volcanos in eruption or of grass growing beside the road we add our understanding—or misunderstanding—of cause and effect. These perceived worlds and events and people are said to be emically structured—structured in relation to the observer, experiencer, or learner.

The perceptions which help build this emic world, and which become part of it, may reach us through touch, sight, hearing, or inner impressions. Each may contribute to the emic product. We may call the whole our referential (emic) world. The perceived world is in part structured through our relations to it.

When we study language, in an attempt to treat it as a partial but not as a completely separate part of our experience, we find it impossible to do so without relation to the referential world. Similarly, we cannot treat or know the referential world without relation to speech, which helps to give it its perceived structure or helps to pass on the knowledge of our experience of this structure to others. In linguistics, then, the referential hierarchy comprises and ties together speech and the world to which it refers.

The linguistic referential hierarchy is seen most easily in a set of paraphrases. Each member of the referential paraphrase set may refer to the same physical, social, personal, conceptual situation, event, entity, or relation.

A stream of speech has a phonological structure, a grammatical structure, and a referential structure. The interface of these three structures is the lexicon—the expanded lexicon from morpheme to discourse. In the lexicon are listed the phonological content, the grammatical class, and the referential value of each unit, large or small.

The sentence 'I'm going' may have a phonological structure with the first syllable 'I'm' unstressed, followed by the stressed syllable 'go' and unstressed 'ing'; but the grammar has the subject 'I' followed by the verb phrase 'm going' or 'am going' as predicate. The referential component includes factors of meaning for each morpheme, and possible paraphrases (in appropriate contexts) such as 'I am leaving now,' or 'As you see, it's time for me to get moving—so here we go.' 'John came home; he ate dinner' is referentially the same as 'John ate dinner after he came home,' although the two are grammatically different.

The referential unit-in-context, like the grammatical one, has slot, class, role, and cohesion. But in the referential tagmeme, the role includes purpose or relevance, whether implicit (deduced by analyst) or explicit (stated by narrator or quoted by actor). The class cell carries one or more members of the paraphrase set naming or referring to some unit in the referential world. The slot cell shows the relation of the item under momentary analytical attention to a larger including situation, conversation, event, or thing, and also indicates its location in time and space. The cohesion cell specifies background beliefs, features, or referential elements serving as controlling or controlled elements of the material being talked about. The level of observer relation under attention will lead to different entries in the cohesion cell, since different observers see things differently, believe different things about them, and may express these observations with integrity or falsely, seriously or in jest. In writing down a text in a langauge previously unknown to us, we employ a phonetic alphabet based on our own experience and that of others. Such first data are approximate only, and biased by the analyst's experience. For an emic or orthographic transcription, more data must be compared with the initial ones, in a search for independent, consistent, contrastive phonological units. Similarly, in analyzing a text for its referential structure, one must begin with a set of provisional judgments of the structure of role, distribution, and cohesion, based upon one's own background. Only later can these be amplified in some areas, pruned of excess material in others, and treated in a more formal emic system as viewed by the speaker of the language being studied. The materials given in the following parts of this section utilize the basic data of Rachel Saint, combined with the general categories and approach of Evelyn Pike, as seen in the classroom, discussing these first etic guesses to a revised, emic judgment.

Notes on Referential Elements in Three Texts

Patricia Wilkendorf

Three Waorani texts are here examined for features relating to the referential hierarchy of language. For each text, an etic list of events is presented, in the chronological order of their occurrence. Among the events listed are (1) all those mentioned in each text, as well as (2) other events which are immediately understood from the text to have occurred and which are also explanatory of the events which are mentioned. In addition, the role (purpose, reason) for each event is indicated. Occurrence cohesion is omitted because more data are needed to know which parts are obligatory and the conditions under which others need not occur. Agreement constraints may not be included especially if they are the same as for a larger including structure.

For the first text (OR), the list of events is followed by a formulaic four-cell representation of the organization of the events according to the viewpoint and purposes of various members of the cast. Such purposeful sequences of events are called 'vectors.' Some of the immediate constituents are developed to single events (those listed in the chronology).

Finally, some of the cast and props (some of the immediate constituents of an event) are presented in four-cell displays. Formulas and four-cell displays of cast members and props have been prepared for all the texts, but because of space limitations are not all presented here. For a more definitive discription of the referential structure of a narrative see Pike and Pike 1983.

1. Referential Elements in 'The Origin of the Rainbow' Story. Here a starting referential list is given, to be amplified or revised. First, the event, injunction, or state itself (equivalent to Cell 2 of the appropriate unit-in-context), then the role, followed by the cohesion, of that same unit.

(a) The ancestors learn all things
    Role: Because of revelation or experience
    Cohesion: Reality

(b) The ancestors pass on this information to descendants
    Role: To help descendants live well or descendants asked them.
    Cohesion: Reality

(b1) The good clay pits are where the rainbow touches the earth
    Role: To find good clay
    Cohesion: Belief of the Waorani people

(b2) Don't point at the rainbow
    Role: Because if you do, your hand will become paralyzed
    Cohesion: Belief of the Waorani people

(b3) Just nod
    Role: To show location of rainbow without being harmed
    Cohesion: Belief of the Waorani people

(b4) Search for the place of the clay pits
    Role: To get clay
    Cohesion: Reality (Do the descendants really believe this?)

(b5) Find clay pits
    Role: To get clay
    Cohesion: Reality (?)

(b6) Bring back good clay
    Role: To make good cooking pots
    Cohesion: Reality

(c1) The descendants search for the clay pits
    Role: To get clay
    Cohesion: Reality

(c2) The descendants find the clay pits
    Role: To get clay
    Cohesion: Reality

(c3) The descendants bring back good clay
    Role: To make good cooking pots
    Cohesion: Reality

(c4) The descendants make good cooking pots
    Role: For cooking
    Cohesion: Reality

Here, the preceding material is recast in four-cell notation and in relation to included levels. First, the highest level treated here, the text itself, may be seen from the viewpoint of its narrator.

Section of their total world knowledge	OR text
To get good clay for making pots	Belief system of the Waorani people

Next, the event may be seen from the viewpoint of the ancestors (the Ancestors' Activity vector). Note that 'Complex' which occurs in a class cell is further broken down.

Ancestors' Activity vector =

PreMar	The ancestors learn all things	Nuc	(1.1) Advice to descendants regarding rainbow and clay pits Cx (b1–4)
Because of revelation or experience	Reality	To help descendants live well	Reality

Advice to Descendants regarding Rainbow and Clay Pits Cx =

PreMar	Location of clay pits (b1)	PreMar	Warning Cx (b2–3)	Nuc	Clay-getting Cx (b4–6)
To find good clay	Belief of Waorani	To avoid harm	Belief of Waorani	To make good pots	Advice of the ancestors

Clay Getting Cx =

Mar	Searching for clay pits (b4)	Mar	Finding clay pits (b5)	Nuc	Getting clay for pots (b6)
To get clay	Reality? (Do the descendants really believe clay pits are at foot of rainbow?)	To get clay	—	To make good cooking pots	—

Descendants Obedience vector =

Mar	Descendants search for clay pits (c1)	Mar	Descendants find clay pits (c2)	Mar	Descendants bring back good clay (c3)
To get clay	Reality clay	To get	Reality	To make good cooking pots	Reality

Nuc	Descendants make good cooking pots (c4)
For cooking	Reality

Finally, the cast and the props are themselves transcribed with four-cell notation.

Close to the origin of the natural world	Ancestors	Far from the origin of the natural world	Descendants
Teacher	Control knowledge and belief system of the whole group	Pupils	Controlled by the ancestors' knowledge of the world

Where rainbow touches earth	Clay pits	Occurs in visible area of Waorani world	Rainbow
Source of clay for pots	—	To show location of clay pits	Waorani view of nature

In clay pits	Clay	Residence where Waorani return	Pots
To make good pots	Properties of that kind of clay	For cooking	Custom (design, shape, size, etc.)

2. Referential elements in 'The Origin of Cassava' story. We now give comparable material, needing revision for emic contrasts and relevance, of a second text—'The Origin of Cassava' story.

- (o) Ancestors learn all things
    Role: Revelation/hearsay
    Cohesion: Reality

- (a) Ancestors pass their knowledge on to descendants (Kadæ)
    Role: Request of descendants (Kadæ)/to show off knowledge/to help descendants live well
    Cohesion: Reality

- (b) Kadæ learns Cassava legend
    Role: Ancestors told him the story
    Cohesion: Reality

- (b1) Kadæ tells his offspring the Cassava legend
    Role: Request of offspring/desire to help offspring live well
    Cohesion: Reality

- (b2) Ancestors have no cassava plant
    Role: Nonexistent as food

- (b3) Ancestors have sweet potatoes
    Role: Grown by the ancestors in order to have food

- (b4) Ancestors eat sweet potatoes
    Role: Grown by ancestors in order to live

- (c1) A man goes hunting
    Role: In order to get food

- (c2) Man (Hunter) looks for animal tracks
    Role: In order to get food/meat

(c3) Man (Hunter) finds many tapir tracks beside river,
and Cassava plants
Role: Tapirs live by river and cassava plants

(c4) Hunter wonders why so many tapir tracks are there
Role: Curiosity

(c5) Hunter leaves (returns home)
Role: Cannot discover reason for tracks being there/other?

(c6) Hunter returns
Role: To investigate tapir tracks/curiosity

(c7) Hunter wonders why so many tapir tracks are there
Role: Curiosity

(c8) Hunter discovers many tapirs live beside the cassava plants
Role: Tapirs eat cassava

(d) Cassava Plant speaks to Hunter
Role: To instruct Hunter

(d1) Cassava Plant asks Hunter to pull up root from the ground
Role: To take home

(d2) Take Cassava home
Role: To prepare cassava

(d3) Peel off cassava skin
Role: To cook cassava

(d4) Cook inside part of cassava
Role: To eat it

(d5) Eat the cassava
Role: To live well

(e) Hunter follows advice of Cassava Plant
Role: To try new food/to live well

(e1) Hunter takes one cassava root home
Role: To try to have new food/to live well

(e2) Hunter cooks cassava
   Role: To eat cassava

(e3) Hunter eats all of the cassava
   Role: Because of Cassava Plant's advice

(e4) Hunter likes cassava
   Role: Because cassava is delicious food

(e5) Hunter goes to get more cassava
   Role: Because he wants to eat more cassava

(f) Cassava Plant gives more instructions to Hunter
   Role: For hunter to live well

(f1) Break the cassava stalk
   Role: To plant it elsewhere

(f2) Clear away the trees and weeds
   Role: To plant cassava stalks

(f3) Plant the cassava stalks
   Role: For cassava to grow

(f4) Cassava grows and obtains leaves
   Role: Because cassava was planted in clearing

(f5) Do not take up cassava root yet
   Role: Because cassava root not fully grown

(f6) Cassava root humps the earth
   Role: Because cassava root is fully grown

(f7) Dig up the cassava root
   Role: To get cassava

(f8) Eat the cassava
   Role: To live well

(f9) Plant the cassava in other clearings farther and farther away
   Role: To have more cassava to eat

(f10) Cassava grows
   Role: Because is planted in clearings

(f11) Waorani people eat cassava
   Role: To live well

(g) Hunter follows advice of Cassava Plant
   Role: To live well

(g1) Hunter chops down trees
   Role: To plant cassava

(g2) Hunter plants cassava
   Role: For cassava to grow

(g3) Hunter clears weeds
   Role: For cassava to grow

(g4) Cassava root forms
   Role: Because clearing is made

(g5) Hunter digs up a little cassava root
   Role: To see if cassava is grown

(g6) Cassava root is still not fully grown
   Role: Because cassava not in ground long enough

(g7) Cassava root becomes big
   Role: Because cassava root is fully developed

(g8) Hunter realizes cassava is now mature
   Role: Because Cassava Plant had told him what it would look like

(g9) Hunter eats cassava
   Role: Because cassava root is full grown

(g10) Hunter tells Waorani people to come for cassava
   Role: To share the cassava

(h) Tapir reacts to Waorani people taking his cassava
   Role: Because tapir wants to keep the cassava to eat

(h1) Tapir realizes there is no more cassava
   Role: Because Waorani people have taken all of cassava

(h2) Tapir protests
   Role: Because no more cassava roots remain

(h3) Tapir cries
   Role: Because he is sorrowful
   Cohesion: Because of Waorani-tapir custom

Hunter Response Cx =

PreMar	Taking cassava root (e1)	PreMar	Cooking cassava (e2)	Nuc	Eating all of cassava (e3)
To try new food	—	To try new food	—	Cassava tastes good	—

	PostMar	Liking the cassava (e4)	PostMar	Going for more cassava (e5)	
	Cassava tastes good	—	Wants to eat more cassava	—	

Cast and props:

Close to origin of cassava for food	Ancestors		Close to time of current Waorani	Kadæ
Teacher/Narrator	Control knowledge and belief system of whole group		Story-teller/Narrator	Controls knowledge obtained from the ancestors

	During time of ancestors	Hunter	Beside the river	Cassava Plant
	Pupil	Controlled by knowledge of cassava plant	Instructor and food	Controls knowledge of how to plant, cook, eat to provide nourishment

Lives beside river with cassava plants	Tapir	Where Hunter clears trees/weeds to plant cassava	Clearing
Victim	Controlled by ancestors' power to take away cassava	Place where cassava plants could grow	Controlled by hunter/ancestors keeping it clear

3. Referential Elements in 'The Jaguar and the Turtle' story. Following the same pattern used for the two preceding texts, preliminary data are given in etic form for the referential hierarchy of a third story. These, like the others, are needing revision for contrast, relevance and consistency of representations, and emic structure in relation to the tagmemic model used.

(a1) The Waorani people live in houses
    Role: For protection from elements

(a2) The Waorani people have clubs and hammocks
    Role: For hunting and sleeping

(a3) The Waorani people name trees
    Role: To identify trees

(a4) The Waorani people decorate clubs with jaguar teeth and claws
    Role: Decoration/show off

(b1) Turtle lays eggs and then leaves
    Role: Instinct

(b2) Baby turtles hatch
    Role: Instinct

(b3) A little turtle grows up with no mother or father
    Role: Instinct

(b4) Turtle has hammock for a home in the jungle
    Role: Because of Waorani custom

(c1) A jaguar comes to the turtle's hammock slung on the tree stumps
    Role: To eat turtle

(c2) Jaguar wants to eat turtle
   Role: Because of hunger

(c3) Jaguar asks where the turtle's mother is
   Role: To see if turtle is alone

(c4) Turtle cries
   Role: Because is afraid

(c5) Turtle says his mother has gone to get jungle potatoes
   Role: To deceive jaguar

(c6) Jaguar asks where the turtle's father is
   Role: To learn if turtle is alone

(c7) Turtle cries
   Role: Because is afraid

(c8) Jaguar asks where turtle's mother is
   Role: To frighten turtle/to see if turtle is alone

(c9) Turtle tells jaguar his mother has gone to get jungle potatoes
   Role: To deceive jaguar

(c10) Jaguar asks if turtle is alone
   Role: To be able to eat him

(c11) Turtle admits he is alone
   Role: Because he decides it is useless to deceive jaguar (?)

(c12) Turtle wonders where his mother went long ago
   Role: Because he is afraid

(c13) Turtle swings in his hammock between tree stumps
   Role: Because is place and time to think

(d1) Jaguar asks turtle to stick out his head
   Role: To eat turtle

(d2) Turtle pulls head in further
   Role: Fear and to protect himself better

(d3) Jaguar becomes mad
   Role: Because of hunger/impatience

(d4) Jaguar shouts at turtle to stick out its head
   Role: To eat turtle

(d5) Jaguar thinks about eating the turtle
   Role: Because he is hungry

(d6) The little turtle has an idea
   Role: To save himself

(d7) Turtle tells jaguar to close eyes and open his mouth and stick out tongue
   Role: To deceive jaguar

(e1) The jaguar agrees to close his eyes and open his mouth
   Role: To eat turtle

(e2) Jaguar closes his eyes and opens his mouth
   Role: To humor turtle

(e3) The turtle jumps down jaguar's throat
   Role: To kill jaguar

(e4) Turtle bites jaguar
   Role: To kill jaguar

(e5) The jaguar groans
   Role: Because he is hurt

(e6) Turtle continues biting jaguar
   Role: To kill jaguar

(e7) Jaguar falls down
   Role: Pain/because he is dying

(e8) Jaguar keeps moaning while lying on ground
   Role: Because he is in pain

(e9) Turtle crawls out of jaguar's mouth and onto ground
   Role: To see jaguar

(e10) Turtle wonders if jaguar is really dead
    Role: Because jaguar is moving

(e11) Jaguar stops moving
    Role: Because jaguar is dead

(e12) Turtle realizes jaguar is truly dead
    Role: Because jaguar is not moving

(f1) Turtle wants to tell the Waorani people about killing the jaguar
    Role: To show off

(f2) Turtle crawls around tree stumps
    Role: To get to Waorani village

(f3) Turtle hopes the Waorani people will come to see
    Role: To show off

(f4) Turtle realizes the Waorani people will not believe him
    Role: Turtles lie

(f5) Turtle goes to the Waorani houses
    Role: To tell Waorani people

(f6) Turtle tells Waorani people about killing the jaguar
    Role: To show off

(f7) Waorani people doubt story
    Role: Turtles lie/past experience with turtle

(f8) Turtle continues to claim story is true
    Role: To convince Waorani people
    Cohesion: Reality

(g1) Waorani people follow trail
    Role: To see if story is true

(g2) Turtle shows Waorani people the dead jaguar
    Role: To prove story

(g3) Waorani people see jaguar
    Role: Proof

(g4) Waorani people believe story
    Role: Because jaguar is dead

(g5) Waorani people jab jaguar with their spears
    Role: To be sure jaguar is dead

(g6) Waorani people take jaguar's claws and teeth
    Role: To decorate clubs

(g7) Waorani people fasten claws and teeth on their clubs to keep
    Role: To decorate clubs

(h) Narrator concludes story
    Role: Because is end of story

How To Know What To Remember
—Affixal Clues

Leoma Gilley

[The combination of affixal features of Person, Tense, and Mode may signal the cultural importance of elements within didactic legends. This cultural importance is related to the communication situation rather than to prominence (Larson 1978) such that the ancestors are communicating group norms and values to each new generation by means of these legends. Sentences marked by a combination of Person, Tense, and Mode—the three together—seem to form the cultural value highlighter on which the rest of a legend is built.]

Sentences Marked by P(erson)-T(ense)-M(ode):   Cultural Values

OC 1	Wẽẽnẽ doodăni æpǽne-ga-dăn(i)-i-pa speak ... -T-P ... -M Long ago the ancestors told this story.	Importance of accepting the authoritative role of ancestors' teaching
OC 12–13	Ayǽ kẽwẽ, Botõ ĭmote, æǽ-ŋĭ-m(i)ĭ-pa take-T-P ... -M Then the Cassava Plant spoke, "Take me!"	

OC 16	õkõnẽ mao, õdapo botõ õdapo æǽ yaa-bi wẽte
	   peel-P
	kǽgadẽnǽ ænõ-ŋĭ-m(i)ĭ-pa
	   cook-T-P ... -M
	When you carry me to the house, peel off my skin, and cook the inside part of me.
		Importance of use of cassava in the society; importance of proper preparation techniques

OC 17	Ayǽ kǽ-ŋĭ-m(i)ĭ-pa eat-T-P ... -M Then, eat it.	

OC 24	*Botŏ yædēmæmŏ ao mă-ŋĭ-m(i)ĭ-pa* 　　　　　　　　break-T-P...-M Break off my stalk.	
OC 28	*Ayæ̆ kæ̆næ̆ wo-ga-kĭ-m(i)ĭ-pa* 　　　　　pull-roll-T-P...-M Then dig up the cassava, *æ̆æ̆ŋĭ-m(i)ĭ-pa* take-T-P...-M Take it, *ayæ̆ kă-ŋi-m(i)ĭ-pa* 　　　eat-T-P...-M and eat it.	Importance of cultivation techniques
OC 30	*Ao ăte, ĭmai ă-ta-pa ăte, æ̆æ̆te mao* 　　　　　　　say-T-M OK, I'll do what I'm told he decided; he took the cassava, *awæ̆ yite, ga-kă-ta-pa ayæ̆ pæ-pa.* 　　　　　plant-P-T-M　grow-M chopped down trees, planted it and it grew.	Importance of planting

OC 36	*Pŏ a-i-dăni, titæ kĕwĕ waa æ̆æ̆-ta-bo-pa* 　　　see-M-P　　　　　take-T-P-M Come see, the tapir's cassava I happily took.	Importance of man over beast—hence the importance of seeing why tapirs now eat twigs and leaves instead of cassava.
OC 37	*Tŏmĕ ĕkayæ̆ go, tŏmăă æ̆æ̆-năni-ta-pa* 　　　　　　　　　　take-P-T-M Later the tapir himself went and saw that all (the cassava) was taken.	

OC 38	*Mănŏmaĭ Kadæ monitŏ, i-mŏni-te apæ-ne-kă* 　　　　　　　　be-P-...　speak-mouth-P *ĕñĕta-mŏni-pa.* hear-T-P-M That's the way Kadæ told us the story.	Importance of intermediary in passing on the advice of ancestors

The mention of the ancestors and Kadæ establishes the authority of the story, and hence its credibility, according to Saint. The instructions for cooking, eating, and cultivating cassava have been passed down from the ancestors and are the exact techniques which are always used by the people. This story teaches the people what foods they should eat, how to prepare them, and how to continue having them available. This story, according to Saint, also explains why tapirs eat leaves and twigs rather than cassava.

In addition to the cultural value highlighter, there are supporting value markers indicated by combination of Person plus Mode and also Tense plus Mode. Examples of both of these value markers are found in the Origin of Cassava story, as seen below.

Sentences Marked by T and M or P and M	Cultural Value
OC 10 — Kīnõ āte titæ nāŋī ē-wa-ta-wo 　　　　　　　　　　exist-food.id-T-M I wonder why there are so many tapir tracks.	Tapir's involvement
OC 18 — Waapōni kabo ī-mo-pa 　　　　　　　be-P-M I am very delicious food.	Use of cassava
OC 30 — Ao ate, īmai ā-ta-pa āte 　　　　　　　say-T-M OK, I'll do what I am told, he decided. OC 33–34 — Ayǣ, ñǣnæ bawa, Mānōmai ā-ta-pa, āte kǣŋātapa. 　　　　　　　　　　　　　　say-T-M Then the root became big. "When it's like that it's mature," the Cassava Plant said, so he ate it.	Cultivation techniques
OC 37 — Wiyǣ wiyǣ wæ-ga-teī-pa. 　　　　　　cry-T...-M "Boo hoo, boo hoo," he (the tapir) cried.	Loss of cassava

In conclusion, it was found that verbs marked with a combination of Tense, Person, and Mode seemed to signal the cultural importance of didactic legends. If the listener remembered those points, he would have a better chance to survive among the Waorani people.

Other combinations were also noted. Specifically, the Tense plus Mode, and Person plus Mode, seemed to support or amplify the highlighted cultural values. When verbs are marked only by Person (or Tense) the content seems to carry the action or storyline.

Some of the values found in the stories studied were: how to cultivate, prepare, and cook cassava for food, how decorations were obtained for weapons, how to harvest jungle grapes, how to PULL OFF a proper deception, who is target for deception, and finally that the end result of a successful deception is the death of a victim.

Tracking Participants at Points Where They Are Not Named

Lynn Zander

[The focus of this paper is on the elements which help keep track of referential participants in two narratives at points where they are not labelled. In general, in reported conversation, the person who is addressed responds. In some instances the context itself dispels the ambiguity in the exchange. In narrative there are contextual clues to the identity of the unnamed participants; semantic appropriateness of a person in relation to an action type mentioned, certain behavior which is to be expected of one and not the other, or person-number cohesion of the verb which may sometimes match one but not both of two participants. When chaining is involved the subject of an independent clause may be the subject of a following subjectless clause—unless some aspect of the context or the predictable behavior of the participants takes logical precedence. These (and other) participant relations affect discourse structure.]

Of many aspects of structure above the sentence level, participant reference is the one discussed in this paper—especially the means of keeping track of participants within the narrative genre. In order to understand Waorani narrative one must be aware of certain grammatical features which help the reader/listener identify the various characters throughout the story.

There is potential difficulty in keeping track of the participants in the narrative discourse of a Waorani text. Although verbs are marked for person and number, subjects and objects need not be overtly stated. As a result, there are many long stretches of sentences without specific statements as to which participant is under immediate attention. (The major sources I have used for concepts lying behind this analysis are Walrod 1977, Gibbs 1977, Schram and Jones 1979, and Thomas 1978. I have made a distinction along the lines of Walrod 1977: a major participant is one who speaks; a minor participant does not have an overt speaking part.)

1. Performative interaction. One problem is to determine the subject of a clause where only the person and number are indicated by the verb. These subjectless clauses are found abundantly in reported conversation. Solution: It is assumed that in an exchange, the person who responds is the same person to whom the initiating dialogue was directed. This is usually simple. At times, however, it may be unclear as to when one person has stopped speaking and when a second person has begun. In these situations I have found no grammatical clues to make things clear. Usually the context itself, however, dispels any ambiguity as to the speaker.

Examples used throughout this paper are taken from the following texts:

>OC—The Origin of Cassava, by Dayuma;
>JT—The Jaguar and the Turtle, by Giketa;
>CB—The Origin of the Corn Bees, by Dayuma.

Pronoun suffixes, as they pertain to this paper, are as follows (Peeke 1973:40).

	Singular	Dual	Plural
1st person	-bo (-mo)	-mōna	-mōni
2nd person	-bi (-mi)	-mīna	-mīni
3rd person	-kā̃ (-ŋā̃)		
female honorific	-dā̃ (-ŋā̃)	-da (-na)	-dā̃ni (nā̃ni)

In OC 29, the Cassava Plant is designated as the speaker. The response in OC 30 is rightfully assumed to be the Hunter to whom the Cassava Plant is addressing instructions.

OC 29 *Mānō-maī kæ̃-mi ayæ̃ wayō-mō   wayō-mō   gab-bi pæ-bo*
      that-like   eat-2 then further-perm.st further-perm.st plant-2 grow-1

   kæ̃-te kẽ-wē, Kẽwē   apæ̃-n(e)-ī.
   eat-ing live   Cassava.Plant speak-mouth.id-be

"Eat it like that, then plant me on other clearings further and further away. I'll grow and eating cassava you will live," the Cassava Plant said. [Cassava Plant speaks]

OC 30 *Ao ā-te ī-maī ā-ta-pa ā-te æ̃æ̃-te mao awæ̃ yi-te*
      yes say-ing be-like say-pst-asser say-ing take-ing carry tree

   ga-kā-ta-pa.
   chop-ing plant-3-pst-asser

"OK, I'll do what I was told," he decided. So he took the cassava, carried it to another clearing, chopped down the trees, planted it, and it grew. [Hunter decides]

In JT, the Jaguar is clearly identified as the first speaker from the preceding sentence. Context gives a clue to the listener by addressing him as "you who swing in your hammock," which could only mean the turtle. In JT 12 the turtle identifies himself by saying "and I am swinging in my hammock."

JT 11 *Bi-tō badā nawāŋa bi-tō badā æ-dō go-dā-ā.*
2-pn mother truly 2-pn mother where go-3h-emph
"Now tell the truth. Where has your mother gone that you lie there in your hammock?" [Jaguar speaks]

JT 12 *Badā īnō kōwæ̆ æǣ-kæ go-dā owo-bo-pa.*
mother over-there jungle.potato take-incep go-3h lie.in.hammock-1-asser
"Mother has gone a little way down the trail to get jungle potatoes, and left me in my hammock." [Turtle replies]

In a further exchange, JT 13–14, the conversation continues without any overt clues in that sentence, but participant is identified by function in the previous context. The person addressed is the one who responds to the question.

JT 13 *Ado-bi-ke kē-wē-mi-?*
one-2-limit live-always-2-?
"Are you all alone?" [Jaguar speaks]

JT 14 *Ado-bo-ke*
one-1-limit
"Yes, I'm all alone." [Turtle speaks]

In OC 17–19, the previous context once more identifies the participants. The Cassava Plant is the speaker. The Hunter, to whom he speaks, responds.

OC 17–18 *Ayǣ kæ̆-ŋī-m(i)-ī-pa. Waa-pōni kabo ī-mo-pa.*
then eat-fut-2-infer-asser good-intens family be-1-asser
"Then eat it. I am a very delicious food!" [Cassava Plant speaks]

OC 19 *Ao.*
yes
"OK, I will." [Hunter speaks]

2. Contextual cluse to the participant. In certain other subjectless clauses, some aspect of the context or the verb identifies the participant or subject. In CB 16, the subject is the corn-bees. In the following subjectless sentence, CB 17, it says 'the contents of his stomach spilled out all over the ground'. The subject is obviously the hunter not the bees.

CB 16 *Kagīŋō-næ ī̃   giwatæ giwatæ kæ.*
      corn-bee   there buzz   buzz   do
      The corn-bees buzzed and buzzed around there. [corn-bees buzzed]

CB 17 *Geogæ æ̃mæ̃-nō-koo   geogæ æ̃mæ̃-nō-koo   geogæ*
      spill   side-twd.another-big.patch spill   side-twd.another-big.patch spill

      go-dẽ-ŋa-kā-ī-pa.
      go-stomach.id-far.pst-3-infer-asser
      The contents of his (stingy fellow's) stomach spilled and spread out all over the place. [contents of man's stomach spilled out]

The predictable behavior of a participant within the known context may give a clue as to the identity of the subject. In the context of the JT story it had to be the turtle that was doing the biting in 25b even though the verb in 24 is also singular but is referring to the jaguar.

JT 24 *Mēñe ā̃āka-pōni   wæ-kā-ta-pa.*
      jaguar over.and.over-intens cry-3-pst-asser
      The jaguar moaned and groaned. [jaguar named]

JT 25 *Wæ-d(e)-ī-ke   mæ̃-mæ̃-mæ̃-mæ̃ pokæ̃-ŋadæ̃-ŋā.*
      cry-perf-infer-limit harder.and.harder   bite-esophagus.id-3
      But the more he howled the more he (the turtle) bit him in the throat. [Turtle predicted by behavior]

3. Suffix clues. There are many instances where the person-number indicator in the verb identifies the subject, for example, where there is a single participant interacting with plural participants. The tapir is singular in OC 37b; therefore, it cannot be the subject of the plural verb in 37c.

OC 37b *titæ Bo-tō kēwē   ā-te   wiyǣ   wiyǣ   wæ-ga-t(e)-ī-pa,*
      tapir 1-pn cassava say-ing boo hoo boo hoo cry-far.pst-ing-infer-asser
      "The tapir protested saying, 'It was my cassava;' and he cried, 'Boo hoo, boo hoo,' long long ago," [Tapir]

OC 37c *ā-nāni.*
      say-3p
      they say. [The ancient ones]

4. Subject-chaining rules. A much harder subject to deal with is finding the participants in subjectless clauses outside of dialogue passages. Sometimes clues are given by the surrounding text if it mentions the participant, or by the particular verb, if it applies semantically to one participant and not the other. When there are no such clues, however, we can sometimes see that the grammatical subject is determined by a discourse-conditioned subject-chaining rule (Jones 1978:272). That is, a certain noun phrase is understood to be the subject of a following clause or clauses.

In JT 22, the jaguar is named as having spoken. In JT 23 'saying' is chain-linked with 'say' of JT 22; so the subject of the following two clauses is the jaguar.

JT 22 *Mēñe Ao ã-ŋã-ta-pa.*
 Jaguar yes say-3-pst-asser
 The jaguar said, "OK." [Jaguar named]

JT 23 *Ao ã-te mõnæ̃ ki-mõ-te æ̃ æ̃-ne-yõ-ŋã ...*
 yes say-ing blink enter-close.eyes-ing open open-mouth.id-when-3
 And having agreed, he closed his eyes and when he opened his mouth wide... [Jaguar]

The naming of an overt subject would take precedence over this discourse chaining rule. In JT 27, the jaguar is said to wiggle, but the subject of the following clause in JT 28 is the turtle, as named there.

JT 27 *Tæ̃. Æbãnõ wæ̃-ŋã-ta-wo ã-te, ayæ̃ ega ega mēñe doobæ*
 plunk how die-3-pst-dubi say-ing then wiggle wiggle jaguar already

 wæ̃æ̃-te õñõ-ŋã.
 fall.down-ing lie-3
 Plunk! The little turtle wondered if the jaguar were already dead. [Jaguar]

JT 28 *Ayæ̃ ega titæke daa go-dõ ti*
 then wiggle turtle crawl go-twd.another alight
 But he wiggled again, and the turtle crawled out and dropped to the ground. [Turtle named]

The chaining rule can also be overridden when the second participant is not named, but when the action which he performs is behaviorally identifiable with one but not the other participant (cf. Section 2).

In OC 6–8, we are told that cassava grows there. The next sentence says 'he/it came away.' From the story we have reason to believe that the Cassava Plant could talk, but none to make us believe it could walk. Therefore, we deduce that it is the Hunter who came away.

OC 6 *Kīn(ō)ăte wa(ă)   titæ ē-wa*
      why   uncertainty tapir exist-food.id
      Why are there so many tapir tracks? I just can't figure it out.

OC 7 *Manō-maī ōnō weka kĕwĕ   mǽ ōnō*
      that-like river beside cassava flat lie/remain
      They are right there beside the river where the cassava grows.
      [Cassava named as subject]

OC 8 *Kīnō ī ă-n(ĕ)-ī-ke   wa-dæ pō-ŋă.*
      What be say-perf-infer-limit away come-3
      Still wondering about it, he left. [Hunter implied as subject]

5. Discourse structure. The ending of a Waorani discourse topic is brought to definite conclusion, and usually the main participant (protagonist) is overtly renamed. Often the one from whom the narrator heard the story—a special kind of participant within the larger discourse context—is also identified.

OC 38 *Mānō-maī Kadæ mōni-tō ī-mōni-tō apǽ-ne-kă   ēñē-ta-mōni-pa.*
      that-like Kadæ 1p-pn be-1p-pn speak-mouth-3 hear-pst-1p-asser
      That's the way Kadæ told us the story. [Kadæ told; we listened.]

In many narrations there is a protagonist/antagonist conflict. Usually the narrator tells the story from the standpoint of the protagonist who is the character that is primarily in focus. In JT 1, for example, the turtle is introduced first. He is in primary focus throughout.

JT 1 *Wēē-nē   kĕwĕ-ŋă-ta-pa   titæke ado-kă-ke.*
      long-ago-in live-always-3-pst-asser turtle one-3-limit
      Long long ago a little turtle lived all alone. [Turtle]

Most major participants are overtly identified by a noun or noun phrase. The only exception I have found is in OC 5 where the Hunter is not identifed by a NP but by a dependent *-te* construction within a verb phrase.

OC 5 *ado-baī ōō-kæ-te   ă-te   go-kă a-yō-ŋă . . .*
      one-like hunt-incep-ing say-ing go-3 see-when-3
      Determining to go hunting he went, and when he looked . . .
      [Hunter]

Prominence of Waves of Space and Time
Timothy Wilt

[Events may be perceived as occurring on waves of space and time. In this suggested scheme, the slot cell contains information concerning which part of time and space waves an event under focus occurs. This reflects tension in a narrative. The idea is illustrated by data from a story about cannibals. Perhaps the most fruitful aspect of this approach is its representation of how tension is manifested in narrative by movement through space and time.]

1. Motivation for placing waves of time and space in the slot cell. Originally, the referential tagmeme's slot cell simply indicated whether the unit in the class cell was nuclear or marginal to other related units (cf. Pike and Pike 1977:371–76; Howland to be published). Using this approach, events marked for person and number by *-ta-pa* would be analyzed as nuclear, and events not so marked as marginal. I suggest an alternative use of the slot cell for three main reasons.

First, I am interested in analyzing a narrative from the narrator's point of view, using her/his references as much as possible. Although a narrator may allow events to be seen from a wave perspective, s/he will not often use the concepts of margin and nucleus in doing so.

Second, the terms MARGINAL and NUCLEAR carry the connotation of value terms such as 'significant' and 'less significant,' 'important' and 'less important' (cf. the use of such terms in Jones and Jones 1979). It may be all right to use these terms with respect to the perceptions of a particular character in the story or the analyst's particular perspective, but it is unlikely that the skillful narrator will include in her/his narration what s/he does not feel to be important for the hearer's understanding and appreciation of that narrative. Thus, rather than saying that an event is marginal—or less significant—than another event, it might be better to simply say that it plays a referential role in the discourse that is different from the more prominent events.

Third, limiting the use of slot cell to the two terms MARGINAL and NUCLEAR does not seem to add much to the description of a narrator's referential structure. I shall now suggest a way to expand the analytical usefulness of this cell.

2. Waves of time and space. The events of a narrative occur within a certain spatial-temporal framework, or field, which is an essential cohesive factor for appreciation of the narrative. Within this basic field, provided by the narrator, events occur on waves of space and time. So, in my scheme, a slot cell will contain information indicating on what part of the time wave and on what part of the space wave the event in focus occurs.

Overt signals of the position of events on the time wave are provided by words such as *ayæ̃* 'then', *woyowotæ̃* 'night', *ēkayæ̃* 'much later', and the suffixes *-ke* and *-yō* both of which may signal simultaneous action. Overt signals of the place where events occur on the space wave are provided by verbs such as *pō* 'come towards a particular reference point' and *go* 'go away from a particular reference point', and be adverbs such as *māniñōmō* 'there' and *iñōmō* 'close by'.

Both the time and space waves seem to control the tension factor of narrative discourse as well as clarify the relationship of events. A brief look at referential function of the *pō* and *go* verbs suggests how this is so.

We have just noted that the Waorani verbs *pō* and *go* indicate an event's position on the space wave. At the same time, these verbs are also used to refer to prominent events. Thus, they exemplify the fact that the same referent may have more than one referential function. Along with contextual factors, the different semantic components of each verb are what enable this dual function. The component of motion enables *pō* and *go* to be seen as prominent events concerning escape and pursuit. The component of direction towards a reference point enables *pō* and *go* to be seen as indicators of an event's position on the space wave.

The second component helps both to create and to ease tension in The Cannibals story. In that narrative, there are three main reference points for the participants' travel direction: the Amazing Screaming Thing, the big river, and the hill. However, the reference points are never themselves referred to before one of the motion verbs referring to motion towards them is used; reference to the event lets us know that something is coming up but we do not immediately know what it is.

For example, E 3 in Figure 1 is *pō-nãni-ta-pa* come.toward-they-pst-asser 'they came toward (something).' With this reference, we know that the event of the Waorani's coming is antecedent to their arrival at a particular physical place in the narrator's mind, but we are not told what or where that place is. Not until the narrator tells of the coming, does he speak of the house to which the Waorani come and of the Amazing Screaming Thing beside it. Then, after letting us hear the Waorani people express fear for their lives (E 4), he says, "They travel fast, come there (pō-nāni 'come they'), stand still for a moment, silently." At this point tension is at a peak. But, with reference to the next event, the tension is released: Around it (the Amazing Screaming Thing) they went (go-dāni-ta-pa) (E 5). Similar creation and release of tension occurs in the telling of travel by the Waorani people and the cannibals toward and away from other reference points (cf. Peeke 1973:13–14, 131–32 for a related generalization of motion verbs). Figure 1 attempts to represent the relationship between these waves of movement through space and time.

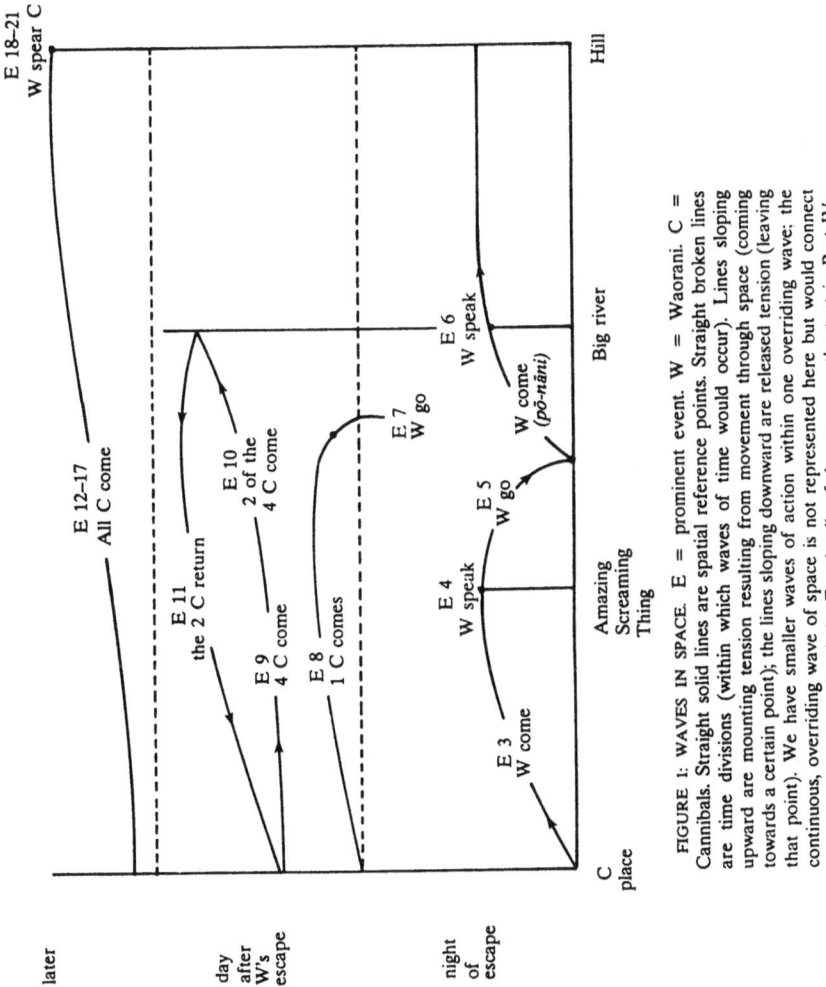

FIGURE 1: WAVES IN SPACE. E = prominent event. W = Waorani. C = Cannibals. Straight solid lines are spatial reference points. Straight broken lines are time divisions (within which waves of time would occur). Lines sloping upward are mounting tension resulting from movement through space (coming towards a certain point); the lines sloping downward are released tension (leaving that point). We have smaller waves of action within one overriding wave; the continuous, overriding wave of space is not represented here but would connect all events in a dynamic whole. For details of the story see the text in Part IV.

Part IV

The Texts

The Origin of the Rainbow

by Dayuma

1 *Doo-dãni Daimẽ go-mõ   a-te,   dai-ka-mõ*
long.ago-3p rainbow go-perm.st see-ing clay-with-perm.st

   mãniñõmõ dai waa-põni ĩ a-te,   daimẽ gõ-ŋæ̃-pa,   ã-nãni.
over.there clay good-intens be see-ing rainbow stand-up-asser say-3p

2 *Ayæ̃ Oo   kæ-mõ-nã-maĩ.*
Then point do-perm.st-neg-like

3 *Oo kæ-mõ-te   a-te   õnõ-mæ̃ kæ-pæ̃-te*
Point do-perm.st-ing see-ing body-arm hurt-arm-ing

   ba-kæ-b(i)-ĩ-pa   ã-nãni.
become-incep-2-infer-asser say-3p

4 *Õnõ-ke okamõ-ke,*
Just-limit head-limit

   ĩnõ a-i,   ã-nãni, daimẽ go-mõ   a-i.
there see-com say-3p rainbow go-perm.st see-com

5 *Ayæ̃ õnõ-po ĩ-te   oo   kæ-dã-maĩ.*
Then body-hand be-ing point do-neg-like

6 *Ayæ̃ tõmẽ-ñõ-mõ   ædõnõ õŋĩ-po põ, tõmẽ-ñõ-mõ*
Then 3.refl-where-perm.st where earth come 3.refl-where-perm.st

   kẽ-yæ̃   go-bi, dai a-te, wa(a)-ẽ-mõ   dai
fast-much go-2 clay see-ing good-exist-perm.st clay

   kæyæ   bæ-kĩ-ĩ   ba-kæ̃-ĩ-pa.
cooking.pot mold-fut-infer become-certain-infer-asser

7 *Mãniñõmõ go-te æǽ-te põ-i-dãni,   ã-nãni, diki*
Over.there go-ing take-ing come-com-2p say-3p everywhere

   diki   diki   mĩ-te.
everywhere everywhere search-ing

8 *Æǽ-nãni-pa, Nawã dai-põni ĩ-pa   ã-te.*
Take-3p-asser true clay-intens be-asser say-ing

9 *Ayæ̃ waa kæ̃yæ̃ bæ-te kẽ-wẽ-nãni-pa.*
   Then good cook.pot mold-ing live-always-3p-asser

Free Translation 1. The ancestors said, "When you see the rainbow in the distance, wherever the rainbow stands is the place where the good clay pits are." 2. Then they said, "Don't point at it. 3. If you point at it your arm will become paralyzed," they said. 4. "Just nod with your head," they said. "Up there is the rainbow, look over there. 5. Be sure you never point with your hand. 6. Then, wherever it touches the earth, quickly go there to that place. Whatever clay you see there will surely be the best clay for making pots. 7. Searching, searching, searching, and going there, bring back the clay," they said. 8. Finding it, the Waorani said, "This is excellent clay!" 9. Then, using it, they made good clay pots.

The Jaguar and the Turtle
by Giketa

1 *Wēē-nē kē-wē-ŋã-ta-pa   titæke ado-kã-ke.*
  long.ago-in live-always-3-pst-asser turtle one-3-limit

2 *Nowa-kã, wããnã wǣpo dae ã   owo-kã.*
  orphan-3 mother father none say lie.in.hammock-3

3 *Kē-wē-ñõ-ŋã,   wa-kã   põ mēñe põ-ŋã*
  Live-always-while-3 another-3 come jaguar come-3

  ñǣnǣ mēñe põ-ŋã põ-ŋã
  big   jaguar come-3 come-3

4 *Owiya(a)-ke põ-ñõ-ŋã   awǣ-tobǣ-koo-dē a owo-kã*
  ridge-limit come-while-3 tree-broken-grove-in see lie.in.hammock-3

  ñaõ kæ-te a owo-kã.
  lasso do-ing see lie.in.hammock-3

5 *Mēñe, Bo-tõ ñõwo ã-mo, Gī-nē ta-ka-yõ-te   ŋawai e-te*
  jaguar 1-pn now say-1 enter-in out-head.id-when-ing seize bite-ing

  a-de   kǣ-mo wæ to-bo-e   titæke ī-pa.
  see-mouth.id eat-1 die laugh-1-permis turtle be-asser

6 *Bi-tõ badã ædõnõ go-dã owo-bi-('i).*
  2-pn mother where go-3h lie.in.hammock-2-emph

7 *Badã ã-ŋī wæ-dõ,   badã ã-ŋī wæ-dõ,   pee pee pee.*
  Mother say-fut cry-twd.another mother say-fut cry-twd.another boo hoo hoo

8 *Badã kõwǣ   æǣ-kæ   go-dã owo-bo,   pee pee pee.*
  Mother jungle.potato take-incep go-3h lie.in.hammock-1 boo hoo hoo

9 *Bi-tõ mǣpo-di(y)æ   ædõnõ go-('o)*
  2-pn father-what.about where go-emph

10 *Mǣpo ēã wæ-dõ,   mǣpo ēã wæ-dõ,   pee pee pee.*
   father exist cry-twd.another father exist cry-twd.another boo hoo hoo

11 *Bi-tõ badã nawãŋa bi-tõ badã æ-dõ go-dã-('ã).*
   2-pn mother truly   2-pn mother where go-3h-emph

12 Badã   īnõ   kōwæ̃   æǽ-kæ   go-dã   owo-bo-pa.
    mother over.there jungle.potato take-incep go-3h lie.in.hammock-1-asser

13 Ado-bi-ke kẽ-wẽ-mi-?
    one-2-limit live-always-2-?

14 Ado-bo-ke.
    one-1-limit

15 Badã   ædōmē̃   go-ga-dã-ī-pa   ã-n(ẽ)-ī-ke
    mother where.might.she.be go-far.past-3h-infer-asser say-perf-infer-limit

    tiigawa   ta-o   wo-o   põ   wo-o
    (name.of.tree) go-away float-away come float-away

    mæ̃netãmẽ-toga   tiigawa-toga   kæ-wo-pa.
    (name.of.tree)-stump (name.of.tree)-stump do-float-asser

16 Ñōō-mē-nē   kæ-wo-kã-ta-pa   titæke
    hammock-vine-in do-float-3-pst-asser turtle

17 Kæ-wo-kã mẽñe, Gīnē   ta-ka-bi   a-bo-e.
    do-float-3 jaguar stretch put.out-head-2 see-1-permis

18 Yoyæ̃ gi-i-ka-te   ã-nē   wo.
    inside enter-away.from-head-ing say-perf float

19 Mẽñe ããka-pōni   pū-n(ẽ)-ī-ke,   Gīnē
    jaguar exceedingly.long.time-intens furious-perf-intens-limit stretch

    ta-ka-bi   a-bo-e.
    put.out-head.id-2 see-1-permission

20 Gīnē   ta-ka   ã-mo ŋawai a-de   kæ̃-mo wæ̃-ŋæ̃ī-pa,
    stretch put.out-head.id say-I seize see-mouth eat-I die-certain-asser

    mẽñe ã-te, ããka-pōni,   mẽñe ããka-pōni
    jaguar say-ing exceedingly.long.time-intens jaguar exceedingly.long.time-intens

    ã-pa.
    say-asser

21 Bi-tõ wæ̃æte mõnæ̃ ki-mõ-te   a-te   æ̃
    2-pn in.turn blink enter-close.eyes-ing see-ing open

    æ̃-ne-te   a-te   yædæ   ta-ginewa-bi
    open-mouth.id-ing see-ing stick.out put.out-tongue.id-2

Giketa: The Jaguar and the Turtle

    a-te   bo-tõ wææte yodã   ta-ka-bo   a-baĩ-pa.
    see-ing 1-pn in.turn protrude go.out-head.id-1 see-like-asser

22 *Mẽñe Ao ã-ŋã-ta-pa.*
    jaguar yes say-3-pst-asser

23 *Ao ã-te   mõnæ̃ gi-mõ-te   æ̃   æ̃-ne-yõ-ŋã   tõ-mẽ-ŋã*
    yes say-ing blink   enter-close.eyes-ing open open-mouth.id-when-3 pn-?-3

    õnõ-mĩka   titæke doo   mĩni   gi-i   wo-kæ̃-te,
    body-throat.id turtle quickly suddenly enter-away.from float-eat-ing

    õnõ-ŋĩnewa mãnĩ ?-?-?   wata wata wata õnõ-ŋĩnewa
    body-tongue.id right here-where-perm.st on.all.sides   body-tongue.id

    mene   wata wata wata mẽñe æ̃mõka   ĩ-nẽ   titæke kæ̃-ŋã.
    for.a.long.time on.all.sides   jaguar inner.throat be-in turtle bite-3

24 *Mẽñe ããka-põni   wæ-kã-ta-pa.*
    jaguar exceedingly.long.time-intens cry-3-pst-asser

25 *Wæ-d(ẽ)-ĩ-ke   mæ̃ mæ̃ mæ̃ mæ̃ pokæ̃-ŋadæ̃-ŋã.*
    cry-perf-infer-limit harder.and.harder bite-esophagus.id-3

26 *Ayæ̃ æo æo æo pokæ̃-ñõ-ŋã mẽñe wææ̃-ŋã.*
    then nip nip nip bite-when-3 jaguar fell.down-3

27 *Tæ̃. Æbãnõ wæ-ŋã-ta-wo ã-te,   ayæ̃ ega   ega   mẽñe doobæ*
    plunk how   die-3-pst-dubi say-ing then wiggle wiggle jaguar already

    wææ̃-te   õñõ-ŋã.
    fall.down-ing lie-3

28 *Ayæ̃ ega   titæke daa   go-dõ   ti.*
    Then wiggle turtle crawl go-twd.another alight

29 *Æbãnõ wæ̃-te.*
    how   die-ing

30 *Kõwa.*
    look

31 *Mẽñe æ̃mæwo wæ̃-ŋã.*
    jaguar thoroughly die-3

32 *Doobæ   wæ̃-te õñõ-ŋã wao-dãni ĩ-nãni go-de   ã-ŋĩ.*
    long.since die-ing lie-3   Waorani-3p be-3p go-return say-fut

33 *Ñõwo go-de   ã-mo,   a-baĩ-(ĩ)-nãni-pa   ã-ŋã-ke,*
   now   go-return say-I see-like-be-3p-asser say-3-limit

   awæ̃mõka-yæ̃ güdãmæ̃ tao   güdãmæ̃ tao ...
   stump-lots   go.round go.out go.around go.out

34 *Æbãnõ æbãnõ kæ-bo ...*
   how   how   do-I ...

35 *Babæ apæ̃-ne-kã   ẽñẽ-kæ-ta-mõ-pa ...*
   wild speak-mouth-3 hear-incep-pst-1p.incl-asser

36 *Nawãŋa-põni ñõwo kæ-bo-pa.*
   truly-intens now do-I-asser

37 *Wao-dãni õkõ-nẽ go-kã-ta-pa.*
   Waorani-3p house-in go-3-pst-asser

38 *Go-te Mãnõ-maĩ Ñæ̃wæ̃næ̃ ĩ-te   wãã   kæ-bo wæ̃-pa.*
   go-ing that-like Ñæ̃wæ̃næ̃ be-ing overcome do-1 die-asser

39 *Nawãŋa kæ-bi-?*
   truly   do-2-?

40 *Bo-tõ nawãŋa ã-mo-pa.*
   I-pn truly   say-1-asser

41 *Õnõ-ke babæ babæ õnõ-ke ã-mi, mõni-tõ põ   ĩ-kæ-ta-mõni-pa.*
   just-limit wild wild just-limit say-2, 1p-pn come be-incep-pst-1p-asser

42 *Õnõ-ke ã-kæ-dõ.*
   just-limit say-incep-twd.another

43 *Nawãŋa-põni ñõwo kæ-bo wæ̃-pa.*
   truly-intens now do-1 die-asser

44 *Ã-nãni-ke, Doo   nawãŋa-põni ã-ŋã*
   say-3p-limit Already truly-intens say-3

   ĩ-nãni-ke, ayæ̃ tõ-mẽ-ŋã nãnõ godõ güdãmæ̃ tao,
   be-3p-limit then pn-?-3   his trail go.around go.out

   güdãmæ̃ tao, õnõ-ke wa(a)-ẽ-mõ-mõni   ẽã   õñõ.
   go.around go.out just-limit good-exist-perm.st-intens exist lie

45 *Mãnĩ-ñõ-mõ-nõ   Ñæ̃wæ̃næ̃ wãã   kæ-bo wæ̃-ta-pa.*
   over.there-where-perm.st-twd.another Ñæ̃wæ̃næ̃ overcome do-1 die-pst-asser

46 *Go-mõ a-dāni õnõ-ke wæ̃mõ-mõni ẽā õñõ.*
   go-perm.st see-3p just-limit beautiful-intens exist lie

47 *Nawāŋa-pōni kæ-t(e)-i-pa,*
   truly-intens do-ing-infer-asser

48 *Babæ õnõ-ke ã-mõ,*
   wild just-limit say-1p.excl

49 *Babæ ã-pa babæ ã-pa ã ī-kæ-ta-mõ-pa.*
   wild say-asser wild say-asser say be-incep-pst-1p.excl-asser

50 *Ñõwo nawāŋa-pōni wæ̃-nõ-nē ī, ã-mōni-pa.*
   now truly-intens die-twd.another-perf be say-1p-asser

51 *Tæ̃nõ-nãni-ta-pa.*
   spear-3p-pst-asser

52 *Tæ̃nõ-te õta baga æǣ-nãni-ta-pa.*
   spear-ing claw teeth take-3p-pst-asser

53 *Mēñe õta kāi kæ-po-te baga kāi kæ-ga-te æǣ-nãni-ta-pa.*
   jaguar claw pull.out do-hand-ing tooth pull.out do-tooth-ing take-3p-pst-asser

54 *Doo-dāni kāi kæ-te æǣ-nãni-ta-pa mēñē õta mēñe baga.*
   long.ago-3p pull.out do-ing take-3p-pst-asser jaguar claw jaguar tooth

55 *Æǣ-n(ẽ)-ī-ke kãta-mõ-ka mã-nãni-ta-pa.*
   take-perf-infer-limit club-big-with kept-3p-pst-asser

56 *Mãnõ-maī mēñe titæke kæ-kã wæǣ ŋã-ŋa-te kãta-mõ-ka,*
   that-like jaguar turtle do-3 down press.tooth.id-ing club-big-with

   ta kãta-mõ-ka wo-dõ-te æǣ-nãni-ta-pa.
   claw club-big-with float-twd.another-ing take-3p-pst-asser

57 *Mãnõ-maī titæke kæ-kã-ta-pa mēñe.*
   that-like turtle do-3-pst-asser jaguar

58 *Tõ-mãā ī-pa.*
   pn-whole be-asser

Free Translation 1. Long long ago a little turtle lived all alone in the jungle. 2. He was an orphan, he had no mother or father, and he was swinging in his hammock. 3. Then someone came! It was a jaguar, a great big jaguar and it was coming closer and closer! 4. While he was coming across the ridge, the little turtle was swinging in his hammock which was slung in a field of tree stumps. 5. The jaguar was thinking to himself, "There's a turtle. I will tell him to stick out his head, and I'll just gobble him up! Ha ha! That will be the end of the little turtle." 6. Coming closer he said to the little turtle, "Where has your mother gone and left you to swing there all alone in your hammock?" 7. "He thinks I have a mother! He thinks I have a mother!" and the little turtle burst out crying, "Pi pi pi." 8. "Mother has gone to get jungle potatoes and left me alone in my hammock." and he cried still more, "Pi pi pi." 9. "What about your father, then? Where has he gone?" snarled the big jaguar. 10. "He thinks my father is alive! He thinks my father is alive!" And the little turtle sobbed still more, "Pi pi pi." 11. "Now tell me the truth little turtle. Where has your mother gone?" the big jaguar growled. 12. "Mother has gone just a little way down the trail to get jungle potatoes and left me in my hammock," the little turtle replied. 13. "Are you all alone?" 14. "Yes, I'm all alone." 15, 16. "Mother! What ever happened to my Mother long long ago?" the turtle thought as he swung back and forth in his little vine hammock that was slung between the stumps of a tiigawa tree and a mænetãmẽ tree. 17. As he swung there the big jaguar came still closer and said, "Stick out your head so I can see it!" 18. The little turtle had pulled his head in still further when he said that, swinging there. 19. By this time the jaguar had become very very mad, "Stick out your head and let me see you!" he shouted. 20. "When I tell him to stick out his head, I'll grab him and gobble him up," the big jaguar thought, "and that will be the end of the little turtle!" And he kept telling the little turtle to stick out his head. 21. Then the little turtle had an idea! "Big jaguar, if you shut your eyes, open your mouth wide, and stick out your tongue, perhaps I will stick out my head." 22. The jaguar agreed. 23. He closed his eyes and opened his mouth as wide as he could. The little turtle took one leap and jumped right down the jaguar's throat there where his tongue was, and bit him again and again inside his throat, first on one side and then on the other for a long time. 24. The jaguar moaned and groaned. 25. But the more he howled the harder the little turtle bit him inside his throat. 26. Then, as he kept biting him, the jaguar fell down. 27. Plunk! The little turtle wondered if he were really dead, but the jaguar was still thrashing after he fell and lay on the ground. 28. Then he wiggled again, and the turtle crawled out and dropped to the ground. 29. "Is he really dead? 30. Let me see." 31. "The big jaguar has finally died!" he realized. 32. "Now that he lies there dead I must go and tell the Waorani. 33. Now when I go to tell them maybe they will come to see," he thought as he crawled around the stumps crawling out on the other side, then around another and out on the other side... 34. "When I tell them how I did it..." 35. "We, having heard, say you are speaking wild..." 36. "It's true, I just did it." 37. So he went to the Waorani houses. 38. Having gone, "Like that I conquered Ñæwænæ and he died." **39.** "Is that so? Did you really kill him?" **40.** "I'm telling you the truth." **41.** "You are just talking wild, you are just talking wild. We are going to go see for ourselves. **42.** You are just making up that story." **43.** "It's absolutely true, I just now killed him." **44.** Since the little turtle said it was true, they followed his trail going around and around the stumps to where the beautiful jaguar lay. **45.** "Right there is the place where I conquered Ñæ̃wæ̃næ̃, the jaguar, and he died." **46.** They looked ahead, and sure enough, there lay the beautiful creature. **47.** "He really did kill the jaguar," they said. **48, 49.** "We were just talking wild when we kept saying, 'You are talking wild, you are talking wild.' **50.** Now we say, 'Truly he is dead.'" **51.** So they jabbed the jaguar with their spears. **52.** And then they took the claws and teeth. **53.** They pulled out the claws from the paws, and they pulled out the teeth and took them. **54.** The ancestors pulled out the jaguar's claws and teeth and took them. **55.** And when they took them they fastened them on their palm-wood clubs and kept them. **56.** When the turtle and the jaguar had the encounter, they pressed the teeth into their clubs, and they fasted the claws on to their chonta-palm clubs, to decorate them. **57.** That's what the Waorani did when the little turtle killed the big jaguar. **58.** The end.

The Origin of the Corn Bees
by Dayuma

1 *Kagïŋõ*
   Corn

2 *Wa-dāni nāŋĩ-mõni kagïŋõ mā-nāni-ta-pa.*
   other-3p lots-intens corn have-3p-pst-asser

3 *Mā-nāni a-te, Põnõ-mĩni kǣ-mõ-e-dāni,*
   have-3p see-ing give-2p eat-1p.excl-permis-2p

   ā-ñõ-ŋā-te, Ba ba ā-nāni.
   say-when-3-ing no no say-3p

4 *Tõ-mē-ŋā kagïŋõ yi-kā-ta-pa, do(o)-po-taa-põni yi-kā-ta-pa.*
   pn-?-3 corn chop-3-pst-asser long-land-go.out-intens chop-3-pst-asser

5 *Yĩ-kā, kagïŋõ nāŋĩ-mõni kǣwipa-baĩ pǣ-ta-pa.*
   chop-3 corn lots-intens cane-like grow-pst-asser

6 *Pǣ a-te, mõni-tõ abǣ-ŋõ a-te kǣ-mi a-te kǣ-mõni-('i),*
   grow see-ing 1p-pn ripe-corn see-ing eat-2 see-ing eat-1p-emph

   ā-nāni-ta-pa.
   say-3p-pst-asser

7 *Mĩni-tõ ba ā-nõ-maĩ kǣ-mĩni-pa, bo-tõ ba ā-mo-pa,*
   2p-pn no say-cont.pst-like eat-2p-asser 1-pn no say-1-asser

   ā-ŋā-ta-pa.
   say-3-pst-asser

8 *Abǣ-ŋõ a-te ado-bo-ke a-de kǣ, ad(o)-õnæ-ke*
   ripe-corn.id see-ing one-1-limit see-mouth.id eat one-day.id-limit

   a-de kǣ-kæ-bo-ĩ-pa, ā-ŋā-ta-pa.
   see-mouth.id eat-incep-1-infer-asser say-3-pst-asser

9 *Ao ā-te ad(o)-õ-næ-ke tõmāā wĩ-ŋĩne-ta-pa.*
   yes say-ing one-day.id-limit all dark-tongue.id-pst-asser

10 *Wĩ-ŋĩne a-te tõ-mē-ŋā kǣ-ŋā-ta-pa, ad(o)-õnæ-ke.*
   dark-tongue.id see-ing pn-?-3 eat-3-pst-asser one-day.id-limit

11 *Edæ,   gōŋa ñō ñō kæ-do-kã ba-yō   ad(o)-ōnæ-ke tōmãã*
   mild.expl fire   lie lie do-out.of-3 become-when one-day.id-limit all

   kapo ka
   entirely cook

12 *Tō-mẽ-ŋã geæ̃-nē-te-baĩ   kæ-kã-ta-pa.*
   pn-?-3   starve-abdomen.id-ing-like do-3-pst-asser

13 *Geæ̃-nē-te-baĩ   kæ-te a-te   nãŋī-mōni kæ̃-ŋã-ta-pa.*
   starve-abdomen.id-ing-like act-ing see-ing lots-intens eat-3-pst-asser

14 *Kæ̃-te, tō-mẽ-ŋã iñōtobæ̃ yidæ   æpo-kã-ta-pa.*
   eat-ing   pn-?-3   suddenly expand explod-3-pst-asser

15 *Yidæ   æpo-te   æ̃-ŋadẽ-ŋã-ta-pa.*
   expand explode-ing go.up.throw.up-stomach.id-3-pst-asser

16 *Kagūŋō-næ ū   giwatæ giwatæ kæ.*
   corn-bee   there buzz   buzz   do

17 *Geogæ   æ̃mæ̃-nō-koo   geogæ   æ̃mæ̃-nō-koo   geogæ*
   spill   side-twd.another-big.patch spill side-twd.another-big.patch spill

   go-dẽ-ŋa-kã-ī-pa.
   go-abdomen.id-far.pst-3-infer-asser

18 *Apæ̃-ne-ga   doo-dãni   apæ̃-ne-ga-dãni-ī-pa   kagūŋō*
   speak-mouth.id-far.pst long.ago-3p speak-mouth.id-far.pst-3p-infer-asser corn

   kæ̃-te.
   eat-ing

Free Translation 1. This is the story about corn. **2.** Others had a whole lot of corn. **3.** Since they had lots of corn, when others asked "Can we have some of your corn to eat?" they refused. **4.** One fellow chopped a corn field; he chopped a whole great big field for corn. **5.** He chopped it and had lots of corn growing, so much it grew like cane in a cane-patch. **6.** They said, "When your corn is grown, and we see it is ripe and you are eating it, let us eat it too." **7.** But he replied, "Since you refused to share with me and ate all your corn, I refuse too. **8.** When the corn is ripe, all alone I will eat it up. In one day I am going to gobble it all up." he said. **9.** Then one day the corn tassels became dark. **10.** When the tassels became dark the fellow ate all his corn in one day! **11.** The rascal! When the firewoood was piled high on the ground-fire, in one day he cooked it all, every bit of it! **12.** He acted as if he had been starved! **13.** As if he were starved, he ate lots and lots of corn. **14.** And having eaten so much, his abdomen suddenly swelled and burst open. **15.** Having swelled and burst open, he threw up contents of his stomach. **16.** The corn-bees buzzed and buzzed around there. **17.** Long ago the contents of his stomach spilled out and spread all over the place! **18.** This story was told long long ago by the ancient ones whenever they ate corn.

The Origin of Cassava

by Dayuma

1 *Wēē-nē doo-dāni apǣ-ne-ga-dān(i)-ī-pa.*
long.ago-in long.ago-3p speak-mouth.id-far.past-3p-infer-asser

2 *Wēē-nē kēwē dæ ā-ŋa-te-ī-pa.*
long.ago-in cassava none say-far.pst-ing-infer-asser

3 *Ā, kēwē dæ ā.*
say cassava none say

4 *Kē-wē-ñō-nāni, kē-wē-te akagæ kōwē ī,*
live-always-when-3p live-always-ing sweet.potato always be

   akagæ kǣ-te kē-wē-ñō-nāni, kēwē dæ ā.
sweet.potato eat-ing live-always-when-3p cassava none say

5 *Kē-wē, kē-wē-te ado-baī ōō-kæ-te ā-te go-kā*
live-always live-always-ing same-like hunt-incep-ing say-ing go-3

   a-yō-ŋā titæ nāŋī nāŋī ē-wa.
see-when-3 tapir lots lots exist-food.id

6 *Kīn(ō)āte waā titæ ē-wa.*
Why uncertainty tapir exist-foot.id

7 *Mānō-maī ōnō weka kēwē mǣ ōñō.*
that-like river beside cassava flat lie/remain

8 *Kīnō ī ā-n(ē)-ī-ke wadæ pō-ŋā*
what be say-perf-infer-limit away come-3

9 *Ēka-yǣ, wææ-te a-kæ go-bo.*
later-much in.turn-ing see-incep go-1

10 *Kīn(ō)āte titæ nāŋī ē-wa-ta-wo.*
Why tapir lots exist-food.id-pst-dubi

11 *Ayǣ go-te ædǣ-mō titæ nāŋī nāŋī nāŋī kōwē*
then going thorough-perm.st tapir lots lots lots always

   kē-wē kēwē weka.
live-always cassava beside

119

12 *Ayǽ Kẽwẽ,*
   then cassava

13 *Bo-tõ ĩ-mo-te ǽǽ-ŋĩ-m(i)-ĩ-pa.*
   1-pn be-1-ing take-fut-2-infer-asser

14 *Bo-tõ yǽwa mãnĩ   õŋipo-dẽ ǽ wo-ga-bi*
   1-pn root over.there ground-in up pull-roll-2

15 *Ǽ wo-ga-bi a-te   ǽǽ-te go-bi*
   up pull-roll-2 see-ing take-ing go-2

16 *Õkõ-nẽ mao õdapo bo-tõ õdapo ǽǽ yaa-bi, ayǽ wẽ-te*
   house-in bring skin 1-pn skin take peel-2 then inside-ing

   kǽgadẽ-nǽ   ǽnõ-ŋĩ-m(i)-ĩ-pa.
   stomach-cassava.root.id cook-fut-2-infer-asser

17 *Ayǽ kǽ-ŋĩ-m(i)-ĩ-pa.*
   then eat-fut-2-infer-asser

18 *Waa-põni kabo ĩ-mo-pa.*
   Good-intens family be-1-asser

19 *Ao.*
   yes

20 *Kǽ-nǽ-ke   ado-dǽ-ke   ǽǽ-te mao ǽnõ-te, a-de*
   cassava-root-limit one-cassava.root.id-limit take-ing bring cook-ing see-mouth.id

   kǽ-te a-te, waa-põni ĩ.
   eat-ing see-ing good-intens be

21 *Ñõwo wǽǽte ǽǽ-kǽ   go-bo.*
   Now again take-incep go-1

22 *Wǽǽte ǽǽ-kǽ go-kã.*
   again take-incep go-3

23 *Bo-tõ ĩ-mo-te mãnõ-maĩ kǽ-bi.*
   1-pn be-1-ing that-like do-2

24 *Bo-tõ yǽdẽmǽmo ao   mǽ-ŋĩ-m(i)-ĩ-pa.*
   1-pn stalk crack break-fut-2-infer-asser

25 *Ayǽ õmǽ wi-yǽ-bi awǽ yi-te   a-te   mĩ-mi pǽ-kã-e.*
   then weeds cut-much-2 tree chop-ing see-ing plant-2 grow-3-permis

Dayuma: The Origin of Cassava

26 *Pæ-kã bo-tõ õñabo ē-a-bo a-te ææ̃-nã-maī.*
   Grow-3 1-pn leaf exist-see-leaf.id see-ing take-neg-like

27 *Ayæ̃ e a-i, tõmãã ēē-ke õñabo ba-bo ayæ̃*
   then wait see-com all finish-limit leaf become-1 then

   õmæ̃ wi-bi, kæ̃-næ̃ õŋipo waa a-bi a-te, pata pata yia,
   weeds cut-2 cassava-root ground well see-2 see-ing (pushes.up the ground)

   mãnī-ñõ-mõ bo-tõ pikæ̃-mo ba-bo
   over.there-where-perm.st 1-pn mature-1 become-1

28 *Ayæ̃ kæ̃-næ̃ wo-ga-kī-mi-ī-pa,*
   then cassava-root pull-roll-fut-2-infer-asser

   ææ̃-ŋī-mi-ī-pa, ayæ̃ kæ̃-ŋī-mi-ī-pa.
   take-fut-2-infer-asser then eat-fut-2-infer-asser

29 *Mãnõ-maī kæ̃-mi ayæ̃ wayõ-mõ wayõ-mõ*
   that-like eat-2 then further-perm.st further-perm.st

   ga-bi pæ-bo kæ̃-te kē-wē, Kẽwē apæ̃-n(e)-ī.
   plant-2 grow-1 eat-ing live-always cassava speak-mouth-be

30 *Ao ã-te, ī-mai ã-ta-pa ã-te, ææ̃-te*
   yes say-ing be-like say-pst-asser say-ing take-ing

   mao awæ̃ yi-te ga-kã-ta-pa ayæ̃ pæ̃-pa.
   bring tree chop-ing plant-3-pst-asser then grow-asser

31 *Õmæ wi-kã, ayæ̃ kæ̃-næ̃ ē-wa-pa ba-pa.*
   weeds cut-3 then cassava-root exist-foot-asser become-asser

32 *Wædæ̃-ke wo-ga-te a-kã ayæ̃ wēēnæ̃-næ̃ ī-pa.*
   few-limit pull-roll-ing see-3 then immature-cassava.root be-asser

33 *Ayæ̃ ñæ̃næ̃ ba-wa,*
   then large become-foot

34 *Mãnõ-maī ã-ta-pa, ã-te, kæ̃-ŋã-ta-pa.*
   that-like say-pst-asser say-ing eat-3-pst-asser

35 *Ayæ̃ wa-dãni ī-nãni-te,*
   then other-3p be-3p-ing

36 *Põ a-i-dãni, titæ kẽwē waa ææ̃-ta-bo-pa.*
   come see-com-2p tapir cassava well take-pst-1-asser

37 *Tõ-mẽ   ẽka-yæ̃   go tõmãã æ̃æ̃-nãni-ta-pa, kæ̃-næ̃*
   pn-refl.3 later-much go all   take-3p-pst-asser cassava-root

   æ̃mæ̃wo   æ̃æ̃-nãni a-te   titæ Bo-tõ kẽwẽ   ã-te
   for.the.last.time take-3p see-ing tapir 1-pn cassava say-ing

   wi-yæ̃   wi-yæ̃   wæ-ga-t(e)-ĩ-pa,   ã-nãni.
   boo-hoo boo-hoo cry-far.pst-ing-infer-asser say-3p

38 *Mãnõ-maĩ Kadæ mõni-tõ ĩ-mõni-tõ apæ̃-ne-kã ẽñẽ-ta-mõni-pa.*
   that-like Kadæ 1p-pn be-1p-pn speak-mouth-3 hear-pst-1p-asser

Free Translation 1. Long long ago the ancestors told this story: **2.** Long ago they had no cassava plants. **3.** There were none. **4.** The ancestors always had sweet potatoes, and in those days they lived on sweet potatoes; they had no cassava. **5.** When they lived that way, just as we do now, someone went hunting; and as he searched for animal tracks, he saw a great many tapir footprints. **6.** "Why are there so many tapir tracks? I just can't figure it out. **7.** They are right there beside the river where there are cassava plants growing." **8.** Still wondering about it, the Waorani left. **9.** Later, he decided to go again to see. **10.** "I wonder why there are so many tapir tracks", he thought. **11.** Then going and looking carefully he saw that lots and lots and lots of tapirs lived right there beside the cassava patch. **12.** Then the cassava plant spoke to him. **13.** "Take me. **14.** Pull up my root from the ground. **15.** Having pulled me up, take me with you. **16.** When you carry me to the house, peel off my skin and cook the inside part of the cassava. **17.** Then eat it. **18.** I am a very delicious food." **19.** "OK, I will." **20.** Taking just one piece of the cassava root with him, he cooked it and ate it all up. "It was very good", he decided. **21.** "Now I'm going again to get cassava," he said. **22.** So he went again to get more. **23.** "This is what you must do to me," the cassava plant said, **24.** "Break off my stalk. **25.** Then after you have chopped down the trees and cleared away the weeds, plant me and let me grow. **26.** When it grows, and you see I have leaves, don't take me yet. **27.** Just wait until all the leaves are grown, then clear the weeds, and when you see that the cassava in the ground right there humps up the earth, **28.** then dig up the cassava root, take it and eat it. **29.** Eat it like that, then plant me on other clearings farther and farther away. I'll grow, and eating cassava you will live," the cassava plant said. **30.** "OK. I'll do what I was told," he decided. So he took the cassava, chopped down the trees, planted it, and it grew. **31.** He cleared the weeds; then the cassava root formed. **32.** He dug up a little to see. It was still not fully developed. **33.** Then the root became big. **34.** That's what the cassava plant said to me, "When it's like that, it's mature." So he ate it. **35.** Then he called to the others, **36.** "Come see! I happily took the tapir's cassava." **37.** Later the tapir himself went, and when he saw that they had taken every bit and that there were no cassava roots left, he protested. "It was my cassava," and he cried "Boo hoo, boo hoo." This is what happened a long long time ago. **38.** That's the way Kadæ told us the story.

The Spider Monkey's Tail
by Giketa

1 *Deye   ǣi ōnō-kagi-miǣ   ōñō.*
  Spider.monkey high body-hair.id-tail.id lie

2 *ōnō tigi tigi pā-da-yō-nāni,   pogodo pō wĩni*
  river slap slap swim-push-when-3p quickly come wrap.around

  kæ-mīka-te   ōŋǣ ōtibæ-bo-dẽ   gi-i-ta-pa.
  do-throat.id-ing grab deep-place-in enter-away.from-pst-asser

3 *Gi-i-te   wãtapiyǣ wǣ-nãni a-te ñĩ-miǣ   kæ-ta-pa.*
  enter-away.from-ing long.time die-3p see-ing release-tail.id do-pst-asser

4 *Ñĩ-miǣ   kæ yidǣ ta-dãni-ta-pa.*
  release-tail.id do swell go.out-3p-pst-asser

5 *Ta,   yidǣ ǣǣ-te wogaa   ta-dãni-ta-pa*
  go.out swell take-ing float.on.surface go.out-3p-pst-asser

6 *Ayǣ ẽka-yǣ,   ōnō pā-da-kǣ-ĩ,   ã-nãni, nãni pā-da-baĩ*
  then later-much river swim-push-certain-infer say-3p 3p swim-push-like

  yǣæ pā-da-te   to-yō-nāni,   pogodo pō bæi   ōŋō-te
  yell swim-push-ing laugh-when-3p quickly come snatch stand,stay-ing

  wĩni kæ-mĩnka-te   ōŋǣ gi-i.
  wrap do-throat.id-ing grab enter-away.from

7 *Ayǣ wãtapiyǣ wǣ-nãni a-te ñĩ-miǣ   kæ ta.*
  then long.time die-3p see-ing release-tail.id do go.out

8 *Wǣ-nãni a-dẽ-nãni ĩ-te, odo odo ōnō-no-ye   bedō ta-pa,*
  die-3p see-perf-3p be-ing less less river-out.of-? drown go.out-asser

9 *Ñõwo bo-tō go-bo ōnō-no-ye   bedō-ŋĩ bo-tō taa-miǣ-kæ-bo-ĩ-pa.*
  now 1-pn go-1 river-out-of-? drown-fut 1-pn cut-tail-incep-1-infer-asser

10 *Ã-nẽ-ŋã   ĩ-te, wa-kã kǣpa to-ga-te   ǣǣ-nẽ-ŋã   ĩ-te,*
   say-perf-3 be-ing other-3 club shave-roll-ing take-perf-3 be-ing

   yægĩkamẽ ke   itǣ   ĩ-ŋã go.
   vine   braid stretch.across be-3 go

11 *Õnõ tigi tigi pã-da-dãni a-te, wa-kã gi-mõ-ŋa-('a)*
river slap slap swim-push-3p see-ing other-3 enter-perm.st-place-emph

yægĩkamẽ tǣĩ-mõ-mõni itæ-dãni õŋõ-ñõ-ŋã,
vine strong-perm.st-intens stretch.across-3p stand,stay-where-3

pogodo-põni põ ñaõ kæ-mũka-te õŋǣ gi-i-kæ-te
quickly-intens come around do-throat.id-ing grab enter-away.from-incep-ing

ã-te kæ-yõ yægĩkamẽ itæ ĩ-ŋã tǣĩ-mõni
say-ing do-when vine stretched.across be-3 strong-intens

gõ kæ ĩ, deye ĩ naimǣ yao õŋõ-ŋã
stand do be spider.monkey be from.behind grab stand,stay-3

12 *Yao õnõ-ŋã, mõŋǣ mõŋǣ gi-i-kæ-te ã-te kæ-yõ,*
grab stand,stay-3 carry carry enter-away.from-incep-ing say-ing do-when

pædæ go-dõ õnõ-kagi-miǣ taa ñǣ-miǣ-ŋã.
extend go-twd.another body-hair.id-tail.id cut sever-tail.id-3

13 *Wǣǣ-ĩ æpǣ-nẽ tæi.*
fall-down-be water-in plunk

14 *Ayǣ gi-i-dẽ ẽka-yǣ a-te ayǣ ado-baiĩ wa põ*
then enter-away.from-in later-much see-ing then one-like other come

edæ, nẽẽ ã-ŋĩ.
mild.expl customarily say-fut

15 *Põ yægĩkamẽ itæ ĩ-ŋã pã-da-dãni põ, yao õŋǣ*
come vine stretched.across be-3 swim-push-3p come grab grab

gõ kæ-ĩ mãnõ-maĩ pæ mã.
stand do-be that-like tight hold

16 *Ayǣ kæ-dẽ-maĩ taa ñǣ-miǣ-ŋã*
then do-perf-like cut sever-tail.id-3

17 *Awǣ-ka ǣi.*
tree-with go.up

18 *Bo-tõ wẽmõka bedõ-te kæ-dẽ-mo-dõ*
1-pn secretly?? drown-ing do-perf-1-twd.another

ã-mũni, nǣka nǣka kæ-miǣ ã
say-2p wiggle wiggle do-tail.id say

Giketa: The Spider Monkey's Tail

19 *Deye ōnō-no wa-dãni ī-nãni*
   spider.monkey river-out.of other-3p be-3p

   wĕmōka bedō-nĕ ǣmǣwo.
   secretly?? drown-perf for.the.last.time

20 *O-maa kōda-ĩ.*
   Empty-place squat-be

21 *Tōmãã ĩ-pa.*
   all   be-asser

Free Translation 1. Long, long ago the spider monkey was sitting up high there in the tree with his long tail. 2. When the Waorani came to swim in the river, the spider monkey would rush out, grab them by wrapping his long tail around their throats and drag them under in the deep water. 3. Then he held them under a long time, and when they died he released his tail. 4. When he let go, the water-filled dead bodies surfaced. 5. Coming up to the surface, bloated as they were, they floated on the water. 6. Then, later on, the Waorani decided to go swimming again. When they laughed and yelled as they always did when they went swimming, the spider monkey rushed in and grabbed a Waorani by wrapping his tail around his throat and pulled him down under the water. 7. Then holding him under for a long time until he was dead, he released his tail and the corpse surfaced. 8. When the Waorani realized that they were dying off a few at a time by being drowned and then surfacing in the river, 9. a Waorani said "Now I am going to the place at the river where the spider monkey drowns them and I am going to cut off his tail!" 10. When he decided that, another Waorani, taking the chonta palm club which he had sharpened, fastened a vine across the river. 11. When the Waorani came to swim he entered the river where the vine was stretched very tightly across the river. Then the spider monkey ran out and fastened his tail around the Waorani's neck and tried to pull him under. But because the vine was tightly stretched across, the monkey was unable to, and the other fellow grabbed the spider monkey from behind. 12. When the spider monkey tried to pull the Waorani under the water, the other fellow reached out and cut off his tail. 13. And it fell into the water, plunk! 14. Then, after that happened, a bit later, another came with the same intention. The crazy monkey! 15. He came, but the vine was stretched across when they came to swim. He grabbed a Waorani, but since the vine was fastened in the same way, they grabbed him. 16. Then, as they did before, someone cut off his tail. 17. The spider monkey went high up in the tree tops. 18. "So you say you will do as I did and grab Waorani to drown them!" he said as he wiggled his short tail, it is said. 19. Never again did the spider monkeys secretly grab and drown others at the river. **20.** And the spider monkeys long ago became dwellers of the forest and no longer lived beside the rivers. **21.** That's the end of the story.

The Spider Monkey's Thumbs
by Giketa

1. *Deye īmaī wēē-nē ē-po-kã-ta-pa, moni-tõ,*
   Spider.monkey this-like long.ago-in exist-finger.id-3-pst-asser 1p-pn

   gatã-maī tæiyæ̃ ē-po-kã-ta-pa.
   woolly.monkey-like lots exist-finger.id-3-pst-asser

2. *Mõnõ ī-po-bo-pa, mē-(y)a mē-(y)a ado-ke ē-po-kã-ta-pa.*
   1p.excl be-finger.id-1-asser two-unit two-unit one-limit exist-finger.id-3-pst-asser

3. *Ē-po-kã a-te yowe wē-ta-pa ado ado*
   exist-finger.id-3 see-ing jungle.grapes dark-pst-asser one one

   yowe be-dãni-ta-pa, nãni be-kã-ī õñõ.
   jungle.grapes drink-3p-pst-asser 3p drink-3-be lie

4. *Pædæ æ̃-po-i, ã-nãni.*
   extend up-hand.id-com say-3p

5. *Ao, ã-ŋã-ta-pa.*
   yes say-3-pst-asser

6. *Pædæ ñæ̃næ̃-ñabæ mē(y)a-baa ga æǣ-n(ē)-ī-ke, Pædæ*
   extend big-bunch two.unit-whole roll take-perf-infer-limit extend

   æ̃-po-te æǣ-i, ã-nãni.
   up-hand-ing take-com say-3p

7. *Ñõwo a-i, yiǣ-ŋã-ta-pa. Mãnī tǣ æ̃mǣwo wæǣ-ta-pa.*
   now see-com peel-3-pst-asser this plunk last.time fell-pst-asser

8. *Awǣpayegõ yi-w(æ)ǣ-ŋã-ta-pa.*
   Thumb cut.off-3-pst-asser

9. *Mãnī tõmãã, ayǣ tǣ wæǣ.*
   this all then plunk fall

10. *Ī-te, deye mãnõ-maī mãnī-mæ-ke ē-po-kã ã-te,*
    be-ing spider.monkey that-like this-many-limit exist-hand.id-3 say-ing

    apǣ-ne-dãni-ī-pa.
    speak-mouth.id-3p-infer-asser

11 *Deye*   *ba-po-kã-pa*   *mãni-mæ-ke, mẽmaa mẽmaa ĩĩ,*
spider.monkey become-hand.id-3-asser this-many-limit two   two   here

ǣmǣwo, yowe   bæ-yõ   wido   kæ.
last.time jungle.grapes divide-when throw.away do

12 *Ẽẽ-ke ba-po-kã-ta-pa.*
finish become-hand.id-3-pst-asser

13 *Tõmãã, ai,   yi-bǣ-te   wido   kæ.*
all   look cut-divide-ing throw.away do

14 *Wẽẽnẽ ĩ-maĩ ẽ-po-ga-kã   apǣ-ne-dãni.*
long.ago be-like exist-hand.id-far.pst-3 speak-mouth.id-3p

15 *Wẽẽnẽ Wǣŋõŋĩ badõ-ŋã, ba-d(ẽ)-ĩ-ke   ĩ-ñedẽ   ĩ-maĩ*
long.ago God   create-3   become-perf-infer-limit be-that.time be-like

mẽ(y)a   mẽ(y)a   ado-ke   ẽ-po-ga-t(e)-ĩ-pa.
two.together two.together one-limit exist-hand.id-far.pst-ing-infer-asser

16 *Yowe   næǣ-po-ga-t(e)-ĩ-pa,   ã-nãni-pa,*
jungle.grapes knocked.off-hand.id-far.pst-ing-infer-asser say-3p-asser

deye   ĩ-ŋã-te.
spider.monkey be-3-ing

17 *Tomãã.*
all

Free Translation 1. Long ago the spider monkeys had four fingers and a thumb just like us and just like the woolly monkeys. 2. They had fingers just like us, two and two more and one thumb on each hand. 3. When their hands were like that, the jungle grapes became ripe and they sucked the grapes that lay on the ground one by one. 4. "Hold out your hands," the monkeys called from the treetops. 5. "OK," the one on the ground said. 6. He held out his hands and the ones in the treetops peeled off two huge bunches of jungle grapes and called down, "Hold out your hands and catch them." 7. "Now look," the monkey said as he pulled off the big bunch of grapes and tossed it down plunk to the ground. 8. As he tried to catch the big bunch of jungle grapes, the spider monkey's thumbs were knocked right off! 9. Like that he had just four fingers left, that's all, the thumbs had been knocked right off. 10. So that's how it is that spider monkeys have just four fingers, they said. 11. After that spider monkeys just had these two fingers and two more—from then on, ever since he grabbed the bunch of grapes and it knocked off his thumbs. 12. They never had thumbs after that. 13. Look, that's all they had. Tearing them off, they were thrown away. **14.** Long long ago the spider monkeys had all their fingers and a thumb. **15.** Long, long ago God created them, and at the time he created the spider monkeys they had two fingers plus two fingers plus a thumb on each hand. **16.** The jungle grapes knocked them off long, long ago. That's what they said about the spider monkeys. **17.** That's the end of the story.

The Tapir

by Giketa

1 *Kḗta ãawǣ   tǣnṍ-ŋã̄-pa.*
  Kenta black.panther spear-3-asser

2 *Kḗta ñṍwo ... ñṍwoṍnæ ãawǣ   tǣnṍ-ŋã̄-pa.*
  Kenta now   today   black.panther spear-3-asser

3 *Ayatia mãnĩ-ñõ-mõ   tǣnṍ-mo wǣ-pa ã-ŋã̄-ta-pa.*
  thigh   there-where-perm.st spear-1 die-asser say-3-pst-asser

4 *Ñãwai   tǣnṍ-mo wǣ-pa   ã-ŋã̄-ta-pa.*
  seize,bite.into spear-1 cry-asser say-3-pst-asser

5 *Ṍõ-mõni   wǣ tǣnṍ-mo wǣ-pa.*
  barbs-intens cry spear-1 cry-asser

6 *Wǣ   tǣnṍ-mo.*
  cry spear-1

7 *Tǣnṍ-mo wǣ-pa   ãawǣ   ã-ŋã̄-pa.*
  spear-1 cry-asser black.panther say-3-asser

8 *Gḗa   næǣ-te go-te-baĩ, Awǣñetǣ wãa*
  Together carry-ing go-ing-like Awǣñetǣ perhaps

  tǣnṍ-kæ-dõ-nḗ-ĩ-pa.
  spear-incep-twd.another-perf-infer-asser

9 *Tṍ-mḗ-ŋã̄ kædiǣ-poni põ tǣ   wǣǣ-pa.*
  pn-?-3   beside-intens come plunk fall.asser

10 *Titǣ bo-tõ apǣ-ne-kĩ-('ĩ)-?*
   tapir 1-pn speak-mouth.id-fut-emph-?

11 *Iyike-ĩ Towa-pade ǣmǣ-maa.*
   Close-be Towa-stream other.side-place

12 *Titǣ, mõni-tõ wḗḗ-nḗ go-mõni-pa.*
   Tapir 1p-pn first go-1p-asser

13 *Ṍkõ taa-w(æ)ǣ-mõni-ke ...*
   house exit-descend-1p-limit

133

14 *Titæ-baī tæ̃nõ-te wī-mõ-ta-bo-pa.*
   tapir-like spear-ing not-sleep-pst-1-asser

15 *Gīta mãnõ-maī waa a-yõ-mõ   nãñi põ-ñõ-mõ   mãnõ-maī*
   dog that-like well see-when-1p.excl bend come-when-1p.excl that-like

   wææ go-kã, ayæ̃ itædẽ tæ̃nõ-ŋã a-baī   boo tæ̃nõ-te, oka-kæ
   guard go-3 then day spear-3 see-like toss spear-ing twist-incep

   ko-ī-mo, titæ nãñi nãã   gi-kapo   ñõ-ŋæ̃-te   wæ̃,
   pierce-be-1 tapir bend double.up enter-knee.id lie-upright-ing die

   wī-mõ-ta-bo-pa.
   not-sleep-pst-1-asser

16 *Ã-mo i-mõni-ke,   Kī-ŋã-nõ   a-kī-('ī)*
   say-1 go.downstream-1p-limit what-game.id-twd.another see-fut-emph

   kī-ŋã-nõ   a-kī-('ī), pogæ̃ka todo todo todo,
   what-game.id-twd.another see-fut-emph hawk   (call.of.the.hawk)

   pogodo mã-wæ̃i   mãŋī   ŋawai i-ka-kã   wæ̃.
   fast   take-downhill bring.down seize bite-head.id-? die

17 *Pãa-te   wodõ-ŋã   i-mõni-ke . . .*
   wrap.in.leaves-in tie.up-1p.incl.incep go.downstream-1p-limit

   a-mõni-ke a-mõni-ke bogi
   see-1p-limit see-1p-limit machin.monkey

   aã   tī-mõka-dã-maī   go-baī ī-kæ-kã-ī-pa,
   call.of.monkey chatter-throat.id-neg-like go-like be-incep-3-infer-asser

   bogi   ñaã wo-kæ-d(ẽ)-ī-ke   tæ̃.
   machin.monkey ? follow-incep-perf-infer-limit plunk

18 *Bogi   wæ̃-ŋæ̃-ī-pa,   i-ka-kã   wæ̃-ŋæ̃-ī-pa.*
   machin.monkey die-certain-infer-asser bite-head.id-3 die-certain-infer-asser

19 *A-mõni-ke kogīkoo   edæ   tæ̃   wæææ̃-n(ẽ)-ī-ke,*
   see-1p-limit grey.furry.sloth mild.expl plunk fall-down-perf-infer-limit

   kogīkoo   i-ka-kã   wæ̃-ŋæ̃-ī-pa,   a-mõni-ke
   grey.furry.sloth bite-head-3 die-certain-infer-asser see-1p-limit

   a-moni-ke, a-moni-ke, a-moni-ke, a-moni-ke, a-moni-ke, a-moni-ke
   see-1p-limit see-1p-limit see-1p-limit see-1p-limit see-1p-limit see-1p-limit

Giketa: The Tapir

    a-mōni-ke, a-mōni-ke, a-mōni-ke, edæ   moõ.
    see-1p-limit see-1p-limit see-1p-limit mild.expl nothing

20 *Kōwatai   māɲi   gīta ǣto-dō-ŋā   kaā*
      wild.turkey bring.down dog jump.up-twd.another-3 call.of.guacamayo

      ǣwǣ,   kōwatai wati,   wāni   go-kā.
      guacamayo wild.turkey hit.of.poison.dart completely go-3

21 *Ñōmǣ-ɲī ī-ñǣ, wǣǣ wǣǣ-mōni-ke.*
      rot-future be-? down down-1p-limit

22 *Iña-nāni, Kī-ŋā-nõ   a-kī-('ī),*
      fellows-2p what-game.id-twd.another see-fut-emph

      kī-ŋā-nõ   a-kī-('ī),   gatā
      what-game-twd.another see-fut-emph woolly.monkey

      a-kī   gatā   a-kī   gatā   a-kī   wǣī-mōni.
      see-fut woolly.monkey see-future woolly.monkey see-fut downhill-1p

23 *Mīkaye, wǣī-mōni-pa.*
      Mīcaye downhill-1p-asser

24 *Moõ   moõ   wǣi-mōni-pa.*
      nothing nothing downhill-1p-asser

25 *Wǣī-mōni, Kī-ŋā-nõ   a-kī-('ī) . . .*
      downhill-1p what-game.id-twd.another see-fut-emph . . .

27 *Wǣī-ñō-mōni, ñōwo-pōni, baā-(õ)næ tōmē nānõ wǣ-ɲī-ke,*
      go.down-while-1p now-intens morning-day himself that die-fut-limit

      mēnaa mēnaa kæ.
      two   two   do

28 *Gīta wīõnõ wīõnõ kæ.*
      dog sniff   sniff   do

29 *Kæ-kā i-mōni-ke,   tāno   tāno   tāno . . . Wǣǣ-ñō-mōni,*
      do-3 go.downriver-1p-limit ahead ahead ahead . . . go.down-while-1p

      wǣǣ-mōni-ke,
      go.down-1p-limit

30 *Mānõ-maī wǣǣ,   tǣ   wǣǣ-pa.*
      that-like go.down plunk go.down-asser

31 Gīta wīōnō wīōnō kæ-d(ē)-ī-ke,   nãnō wææ̃-mō-nikæ̃
    dog sniff sniff do-perf-infer-limit that descend-1p.excl-stream.id

    gamæ̃nō æ̃i   wææ̃-mōni-ke,
    toward ascend descend-1p-limit

32 Gīta mēñe kæ̃-ŋã wæ̃-ŋī.
    dog jaguar eat-3 die-fut

33 Gīta, gīta, pē-mōni wææ̃-ŋã ī-mōni-ke,   kæ̃i
    dog dog call-1p descend-3 go.downriver-1p-limit cassava.dough

    ū-padikæ̃ kōnō-te pō be-kī-ī-pa.
    this-stream set-ing come drink-fut-infer-asser

34 Tækægidē ī-ta-pa   kō kæ-mōni.
    Half.way be-pst-asser set do-1p

35 Mānō-maī mæ̃i wī ōnō-ŋã, ū te te mō-ke pō, ūmōñō
    That-like take.up ? smell-3 here step step sleep-just come yesterday

36 Bo-tō æ̃i-d(ē)-ī-ke   pogæ̃ka ī-maī kæ-te ka-ta-pa.
    1-pn go.up-perf-infer-limit hawk   be-like do-ing bite-head.id-pst-asser

    Pogæ̃ka i-ka-kæ   kæ-pa ã-te, waa a-yō-mo, gū-yō
    hawk bite-head.id-incep do-asser say-ing well see-when-1 enter-when

    pæ̃tikoo wi kæ-kæ-te wãa e   a-dē-mo e-te   a gō-ñō-mo.
    leaves cover do-incep-ing perhaps desist see-perf-1 bite-ing see set-when-1

37 Wīoŋō wīoŋō kæ-d(ē)-ī-ke,   pogodo gii-yō,   gīta aoo ã go-de
    sniff sniff do-perf-infer-limit quickly enter-when dog howl say go-return

    pō-nē-ñō-mō,   ōnōke ōmēta   gãni gãni gãni
    come-perf-when-1p.excl just underbrush crooked crooked crooked

    tōmē-ñō-mō   yiæ̃ yiæ̃, Kæ̃mæ̃ kæ̃yæ̃-mōni
    right.there-where-perm.st ? ?   Kæmæ fast-intens

    kæ-bã-we   ã-mo.
    do-urgent.com-remon say-I

38 Æ̃æda æ̃æda æ̃æda wæ̃i-kã wæ̃ī-mōni.
    bend bend bend descend-3 go.downhill-1p

39 Botō, Īi kē-wē-ñō-mō ...
    1-pn here live-always.id-where-1p.excl

Giketa: The Tapir

40 *Kǣmǣ̃, Ǣæ go-de pō-nē-te,   wæ-kã wæ-d(ē)-ī-ke,*
   Kǣmæ Oh! go-return come-perf-ing cry-3 cry-perf-infer-limit

   Kīn(ō)āte wæ-kã ã-te mōnō pogodo gii-ga-dē bo-tõ ī-mo-te
   why   cry-3 say-ing 1p   quickly enter-swamp-in 1-pn be-1-ing

   pogodo wǣǣ̃ ōnōkado-pōni gãñī-kado ī-mǣ̃   ã-ŋē-nē
   quickly descend nose-intens short-nose.id this-side say-admon-perf

   biyǣ̃-ka-te   kade   wodōka-te   ōŋǣ̃.
   lowered-head.id-ing piggy.back carry.backwards-ing lift

41 *Pogodo mao   bæ   ta-te   wǣǣ̃-to-dō-ŋã̄   go.*
   Quickly come.toward knocked over-ing down-straight-twd.another-3 go

42 *Kǣmǣ̃, Badogaa, taadō-ke wǣi-bawe,   ã-ŋã̄ wǣd(ē)-ī-ke,*
   Kǣmæ Look.at.that! trail-limit downhill-urgent.com say-3 cry-perf-infer-limit

   bo-tō teta   teta teta teta teta . . . . Kēyǣ̃-mōni ǣ̃.
   1-pn step.in.water   Fast-intens go.upriver

43 *Eamōka   ea-mōka   īñōmō, dæ.*
   listen-ear.id listen-ear.id there none

44 *Ǣmōŋa-yedē   mǣ̃i   oo oo oo.*
   top-at.that.time go.to.top yelp.of.dog

45 *Ayǣ̃ kēyǣ̃ gatā-koo-dē   mǣ̃i   gīta ī-ŋã̄   gǣ̃ǣ̃pi*
   then fast long.grass-patch-in go.to.top dog be-ing left.behind

   gatā   pædæ wǣi   gīta ōmake   ǣ̃i   wioŋō.
   long.grass extend downward dog in.the.underbrush go.up sniff

46 *Titæ-ke ǣ̃i-yō   mǣ̃i   a-te   aoo ã-ŋã̄ nãñi*
   titæ-limit go.up-when go.to.top see-ing howl say-3 bend

   pō-ñō-mō   tee.
   come-when-1p.excl step.carefully

47 *Ayǣ̃ wātæ wātæ ī-ñō   ǣ̃mǣ̃-maa   mǣ̃i,*
   then shortly shortly be-when other.side-place go.to.top

   oo oo, ǣ̃-mō-ŋa-yedē   poo.
   yelp   up-perm.st-place-at.that.time splash

48 *Ayǣ̃ ǣ̃-mō-ŋa-tibæ,   oo*
   then up-perm.st-deep.spot yelp

49 *Adogaatǽ gãmǽnõ mǽi poo.*
   circle.around toward go.to.top splash!

50 *Adogaatǽ gãmǽnõ . . .*
   circle.around toward

51 *Kǽmǽ tõnõ Yiko ǽ-ñõ-na, Æǽ, i-dẽ põnẽ-te,*
   Kæmæ and Yiko go.up-when-3d so go.downriver-perf think-ing

   w(æ)ǽ-ñõ-na teee.
   go.down-when-3d step.carefully

52 *Ayǽ teta teta teta teta. Nãñiwǽ nãñiwǽ ǽi, taadõ-mõni wǽæ*
   then stepping.in.water around.bend around.bend go.up trail-intens guard

   wãnõ-ŋã gõ-ŋǽ.
   lie.in.wait-3 stand-upright

53 *Mõni-tõ wæǽ i-mõni.*
   1p-pn go.down go.downriver

54 *Bo-tõ wæǽ i-yõ-mõ adogaatǽ gãmǽnõ wæǽ,*
   1-pn go.down go.downriver-when-1p.excl circle.around toward go.down

   iña-na Yææææ i-dẽ põnẽ-te wæ-da . . .
   dear.ones-3d yell go.downriver-perf think-ing cry-3d

55 *Mõni pū-te wǽ-ŋī-ke.*
   1p.excl mad-ing die-fut-limit

56 *Õŋõ-i-da, gīta-idi yao õŋõ-i-da õŋõ-mīna-te titæ-ke ba-yõ*
   hold-!-2d dog-group grab stay-!-2d stay-2p-ing tapir-limit become-when

   tǽnõ-mo-e-da ã a-pa, ã-ñõ-mo, Yao õŋõ-kæ kæ-yõ-mõna
   spear-1-permis-2d say see-asser say-when-1 grab hold-incep do-when-1d

   tõmẽ pokǽ-kæ kæ wæ-d(ẽ)-ī-ke ea-mõna-pa, ã-na.
   themselves bite-incep do cry-perf-infer-limit be.careful-1d-asser say-3d

57 *Wǽpo wǽ-kæ-kã-ī-pa kẽ-wẽ-mīna bo-tõ ã-mo.*
   your.father die-incep-3-infer-asser live-always.id-2d 1-pn say-1

58 *Yǽnǽmõ-koo-dẽ gãmǽnõ, titæ yǽnǽmõ-koo-dẽ*
   briar-patch-in toward tapir briar-patch-in

   gi-i-d(ẽ)-ī-ke ææ gãtite nǽ gõŋǽ.
   enter-away.from-perf-infer-limit stand.up stand.up-ing stop stand.upright

Giketa: The Tapir

59 *Nãnõ gi-i-ke mãɲi, õnõ-todepæ̃ æ̃mæ̃nõ õnõ-todepæ̃.*
 that enter-away.from-limit come body-thigh other.side body-thigh

 Wãtæ wãtæ pokæ̃-ŋã wæ-d(ẽ)-ĩ-ke godomẽnõ ɲãmæ̃.
 shortly shortly bite-3 cry-perf-infer-limit fled.fast himself

60 *Awæ̃-mõ-kado, edæ, awæ̃-mõ-nẽne nãnõ wæ̃-ŋĩ-ke.*
 tree-perm.st-nose mild.expl tree-perm.st-beside that die-fut-limit

61 *Bo-tõ pogodo-põni wæ̃æ̃ i-bo Awæ̃-mõ-nẽne,*
 1-pn fast-intens descend come.downriver-1 tree-perm.st-beside

 wæ̃æ̃-ñõ doobæ bobæ̃ŋaimõ-nẽne giidãmæ̃ tadõmẽmõ
 descend-when already kapok.log-beside go.around come.out.other.side

 gõŋæ̃-ñõ, guĩta mãɲĩ wææ wanõ æo pokæ̃-ŋã pokæ̃-ŋã
 stay.upright-when dog take.down guard lie.in.wait nip bite-3 bite-3

 giidãmæ̃ tadõmẽ-ke ãawẽnẽta tadõmẽmõ
 go.around come.out.other.side-limit ? come.out.other.side

 gõŋæ̃-ñõ, giidãmæ̃ tadõmẽmõ taa, gãnipiyæ̃ gãnipiyæ̃
 stay.upright-when go.around come.out.other.side come.out crooked crooked

 põ-ĩ-mõ põ. Tadõmẽ-mæ̃ põ ayatãka-miæ̃ka pokæ̃-kæ
 come-be-? come come.out.other.side-land come pull.with-tail.with bite-incep

 pokæ̃-ŋã põ. Tadõmẽ-ke taa-yõ
 bite-3 come come.out.other.side-limit come.out-when

 tækæi-dẽ-mæ̃-põni wa ti, ayæ̃ okæ okæ kõ-ñõ-mo
 in.the.side-halfway-intens hit.with.spear ? then wiggle wiggle pierce-when-1

 bige-te bige-te ta(a)-yõ, mæ̃ pokæ̃ mæ̃ pokæ̃ æpæ̃-nẽ tæi.
 weak-ing weak-ing come.out-when hard bite hard bite water-in splash

62 *Bo-tõ õnõ-kagĩmiæ̃ yao õŋõ toõ.*
 1-pn body-tail grab catch pull.straight

63 *Bado, Kæ̃mæ̃ õŋõ-mã-we ã-mo, guĩta toõ godõ-ŋã.*
 Hey! Kæmæ catch-!-remonst say-1 dog pull.straight go.toward-3

64 *Titæ-ke okã-to-ka okæ okæ ko-ĩ-mo tõmææ-wæ̃*
 tapir-limit short-stick.id-with twist twist pierce-be-1 exhausted

 bige-te bige-te bige-te . . .
 weak-ing weak-ing weak-ing . . .

65 *Æpǣ-nē ǣi-yō,*
   water-in go.upriver-when

   õta dika-ka go-dõ tæi tæi ta-ka-bo, õñæ kayæi
   stick stone-with throw bang bang hit-head.id-1 fell.over ???

66 *Edæ, wæǣi edæ.*
   mild.expl descend mild.expl

67 *Kǣmǣ, Doobæ wǣ-pa mo.*
   Kæmæ already die-asser ?

68 *Kǣmǣ ñĩpo kækã toõ   godõ toõ   godõ apǣ-tibæ po-wæ*
   Kæmæ let.go do-3 straight pull straight pull water-deep going.under

   tade   gi-i   powæ   tade   gi-i   pokǣ.
   blow.out enter-away going.under blow.out enter-away bite

69 *Tadõmẽŋadǣ ǣnõwæǣmǣ.*
   underneath   upside.down

70 *Bæi õŋõ ǣ-mõni-ke   wiyãã, mãnĩ   tǣ,*
   grab stay come.upriver-1p-limit drag bring.downstream plunk

   wiǣ-mõni-pa.
   cut.up-1p-asser

71 *Kǣmǣ ĩ-te   õnõke titæ bæ   ta, Kǣmǣ betamõka*
   Kæmæ be-ing just tapir knock over Kæmæ sideways

   gi-i   tǣ   go-w(æ)ǣ-pa.
   enter-away plunk go-down-asser

72 *Bo-tõ-ke ĩ-mo wodõka-te   æǣ-te go-pa titæ titæ bo-tõ ĩmo*
   1-pn-limit be-1 lift.backwards-ing take-ing go-asser tapir tapir ?-pn be

   kadi   wo-kæ-te õŋǣ, mõŋǣ mõŋǣ titæ go-pa
   piggy.back carry-?-ing catch carry carry tapir go-asser

73 *Mãnõ-maĩ mao bææ taa tǣ   go-w(æ)ǣ-te, bo-tõ æǣyǣ*
   that-like come knock over plunk go-down-ing 1-pn ?

   gãti-bo-pa.   Æǣyǣ gãti-te   mao togǣ-te   titæ wã   tǣnõ-mo
   stand.up-1-asser ? stand.up-ing carry sharpen-ing tapir finally spear-1

   wǣ-pa.
   die-asser

Giketa: The Tapir

Free Translation 1. Kenta speared a black panther. 2. Kenta now . . . today speared a black panther. 3. "In the thigh, right there, I speared him," he said. 4. "The dulled spear tore him and he howled. 5. The barbed notches went down in when I speared him again, and he growled. 6. He moaned and I jabbed in my spear. 7. I speared the black panther and he groaned." 8. If Kenta and Awæñetæ had gone together carrying their weapons perhaps Awæñetæ would have speared the black panther. 9. It came toward them and fell down dead right beside them. 10. Shall I tell you about the tapir? 11. It happened not far from here on the other side of Towa's stream. 12. When we encountered the tapir, some of us went first. 13. As we left the house and went downhill, I told the others about my dream. 14. I dreamed that I speared a tapir. 15. In my dream when I looked carefully around the bend of the river, it was as if I saw the dog holding the tapir at bay. I dreamed that when daylight dawned it was as if I jabbed in my spear and twisted it around and around until the tapir fell down dead to the ground and lay there with his hoofs doubled up under him. 16. I was telling my dream as we went downriver. We kept on the lookout constantly for game. We heard a hawk call "Todo, todo, todo." The dog dashed downhill fast after it, brought it down, seized the hawk and bit it on the head and killed it. 17. We wrapped it in leaves and hung it up on a limb, and we came on downriver watching for game as we came. We couldn't hear the call of the machin monkey; but the dogs must have heard it, for they followed it and brought it down. 18. The bogi monkey will certainly die. The dogs will bite its head; it will surely die. 19. As we watched for game, Whoops! a woolly grey sloth fell right at our feet. "That one has been fatally bitten too," we said. So we went on searching, searching, searching for game. Oops! Another one, but we missed it! 20. A wild turkey was in the forest. The dog chased it. It flapped its wings and sat on a limb. We shot it with a poisoned dart, but it disappeared. 21. That one will rot in the forest, we decided, and we went on downriver. 22. "Say, fellows, let's go on downriver looking for woolly monkeys. 23. Minkaye, let's go on downhill." 24. We went on downhill, but didn't get a thing. 25. We went on down searching for whatever game we could find. 26. As we were going down, suddenly we got excited. Those tracks were made recently just this morning. That tapir is as good as dead! You can see the footprints clearly, two and two! 27. The dogs began to sniff. 28. As they sniffed, we followed them on down. There before us we could see where it went. 29. When we went down, as we were on the way, Kenta said 30. "See where the tapir fell down." 31. The dog began to sniff, so we followed it down toward the stream where the tapir had gone, up the other side and down to the next stream. 32. "A jaguar will kill the dog and eat it", we thought. 33. So we called and called to the dog as we went down to the stream and on downriver. On the way we said,

"Let's leave the prepared cassava at the stream so we can drink it when we come back." 34. It was just about halfway, so we set the packages of prepared cassava there. 35. There where the ground was mashed the dog sniffed. I said, "Here are the tapir's footprints where he came to sleep. Here is where he slept last night." 36. As I went up the other side, I thought it looked as if the dog had hunted down a hawk. But when I got closer, I looked carefully, setting aside the small leaf of the palm. Then I covered over the nest with the leaves again so nothing would happen to the young. 37. As the dog sniffed some more, suddenly he dashed into the forest barking and came out again. When I thought about it, I decided that the tapir had just gone into the weeds. Then the dog started snapping at the tapir! It was right there, and the dog was on its heels! "Kæmæ, hurry. Come quick," I said. 38. It was getting later and later in the afternoon, and we went further and further downhill. 39. "I'm going to wait here", I said. 40. Then Kæmæ yelled, "Oh! It's coming back. What am I going to do?" Wondering why she was yelling, the rest of us quickly entered the swampy jungle. Just then the tapir headed straight for me with his short snout. With his head down he charged between my legs, lifted me up, and carried me piggy back—backwards! 41. The others dashed to the rescue, but the tapir knocked them over! Then he threw me off and raced on! 42. Kæmæ yelled at me, "Hurry! Run down the trail fast!" So I went racing off down the trail. "I will have to go fast up the other side," I said to myself. 43. I kept listening for the tapir, but I heard nothing there. 44. By the time I got to the top of the hill, I heard the dog yelping again. 45. But the tapir dashed into the weeds at the top of the hill fast, leaving the dog behind, and went down the other side, but the dog went up through the underbrush sniffing as he went. 46. Then the dog saw the tapir alone at the top of the hill and barked again. Just then, the tapir came around the bend of the river in the water. 47. Then, a few minutes later, the dog crossed to the other side and went to the top of the hill, barking as he went. At the time he reached the top, the tapir splashed into the water. 48. Upriver in the deep part the dog barked again. 49. The tapir went around in a circle and splashed into the water again. 50. Then around again... 51. About that time Yico and Kæmæ came upriver. Aæ! Thinking it was downriver, they both went downriver. 52. Then, running around the bends of the rivers, I hurried upriver as fast as I could. Right on the trail the dog was standing there holding the tapir at bay. 53. We went down to the river again and headed downstream. 54. When I went down to the stream and headed back downriver circling round and going down, the two girls yelled thinking it had gone downstream so they cleared out of that area! 55. We were so mad at the tapir we said, "It's as good as dead!" 56. I said, "Both of you grab the dogs; just let me spear that tapir by itself." When I said that, they called back, "When we try to grab the dogs, the dogs themselves try to bite us; so we can't do it!" **57.** I said to them, "Your father is about to die, I tell you, and you are doing nothing about it!" **58.** The tapir headed for the briar patch; and just as he was about to enter it, he just stopped and stood there. **59.** As the tapir was about to enter, the dogs came toward him and bit him first on one leg and then on the other; but just a few minutes later the tapir himself fled. **60.** Then the tapir ran beside a fallen log. "Oh boy! That will be the end of him!" I thought. **61.** Swiftly running down to the stream, I headed back downriver. By the time I got to the old felled kapok tree log and had gone around to the other side and stood there, the dog was keeping the tapir at bay. The tapir too was threatening the dog. As the dog was trying to bite the tapir's rump, going around to the other side, I speared him right under the fore-leg. When I poked in the spear, twisting it around and around—when I did that, the tapir came out in the open exhausted, the dog biting him fiercely all the time until he fell in the water! **62.** I pulled the dog back by his tail. **63.** "Quick, Kæmæ, grab the dog," I said, so she pulled the dog back. **64.** I speared the tapir again and again with the short spear, and he stumbled into the underbrush half dead. **65.** When I went a bit farther upriver, I threw sticks and stones at his head until he fell over. **66.** "Look at that! He fell over! Just look at that! **67.** He's fallen down dead. He's not moving," Kæmæ said. **68.** Kæmæ let go the dog and he dashed to the deep water, going under and blowing out the water as he bit the fallen tapir. **69.** It was on its back, feet up. **70.** I grabbed it and dragged it over, and we began to butcher it. (Additional information given by Giketa upon guestioning) **71.** The tapir just knocked over Kæmæ, she was knocked sideways. **72.** I was the one the tapir took off. He lifted and carried me piggyback as he ran. **73.** When the others came and kicked the tapir, I fell off. Then I got up again to my feet. **74.** I followed the tapir and finally finished him off with my spear.

The Alligator and the Bird
by Giketa

1 *Nõma wẽẽ-nẽ põ-te, waa a-kã, biwü a õtokado õŋõ.*
  Alligator long.ago-in come-ing good see-3 bird see limb stand

2 *Kĩn(õ)āte bi-tõ kǣ-nã-maĩ kẽ-wẽ-mi-(í).*
  why 2-pn eat-neg-like live-always-2-emph

3 *Kõ-wẽ mãnõ-maĩ kẽ-wẽ-mo.*
  ?-always that-like live-always-1

4 *Bo-tõ bi-tõ ĩ-mi-te mãnõ-maĩ ã-mo.*
  1-pn 2-pn be-2-ing that-like say-1

5 *Bo-tõ tõ-nõ, bi-tõ wǣi-po-dē bo-tõ õntokado õŋõ-mo*
  1-pn and-twd.another 2-pn down-earth.id-in 1-pn limb stand-1

  a, bi-tõ kǣ-nã-maĩ, me-(y)a wa-depo a-te kǣ-ŋĩ-mõna.
  see 2-pn eat-neg-like two-together another-year.id see-ing eat-fut-1d

6 *Nõma ao ã*
  alligator yes say

7 *Bo-tõ kǣ-nã-maĩ ado-baĩ ĩ-mo.*
  1-pn eat-neg-like one-like be-1

8 *Ao ã-na-ta-pa.*
  yes say-3d-pst-asser

9 *Ao ã-te a, nõma mõ ñõ-ŋã.*
  yes say-ing see alligator sleep lie-3

10 *Itǣdē woyowotǣ ñani omǣ-mõ-te a-d(ē)-ĩ-ke a,*
   day night recline awake-sleep-ing see-perf-infer-limit see

   mõ ñõ-ŋã.
   sleep,close.eyes lie-3

11 *Ayǣ, ǣbãnõ biwü kǣ-kã-ta-wo ã-te,*
   then how bird do-3-pst-dubi say-ing

   nõma ñani õmǣ-mõ-te ǣ-mõ a-kã
   alligator recline awake-sleep-ing up-perm.st see-3

145

12 Õtoka a,   odæ   āa-d(ē)-ī-ke   go-mõ-ŋaá
   stick   see pick bathe-perf-infer-limit go-perm.st-loc-see

13 Nõma mõ   ñõ-te ããka
   alligator sleep,close.eyes lie-ing exceedingly.long.time

   õñõ-te, æbãnõ biwü kæ-kã-ta-wo ã-te,   æ̃-mõ   a-kã.
   lie-ing how   bird do-3-pst-dubi say-ing up-perm.st see-3

14 Ayæ̃ odæ āa-dẽ.
   then pick bathe-perf

15 Bo-tõ ayæ̃ ado-ba(ī)ī-ŋã õŋõ-mo-pa, ã-te,
   1-pn then one-like.be-3 stand-1-asser say-ing

   nõma   æ̃-mõ   a-kã, ayæ̃ a, odæ āaī-ŋã
   alligator up-perm.st see-3 then see pick bathe.be-3

16 Āãka   õñõ-n(ē)-ī-ke   nõma   mõ   ñõ-ñõ-ŋã to   mao
   exceeding.long.time lie-perf-infer-limit alligator sleep lie-while-3 straight bring

   kæ̃-te põ   tæ̃,   to   mao kæ̃-te põ   tæ̃,   to   mao kæ̃-te
   eat-ing come perch straight bring eat-ing come perch straight bring eat-ing

   põ   tæ̃,   to   mao kæ̃-te põ   tæ̃   kæ̃.
   come perch straight bring eat-ing come perch eat

17 Nõma   õñõ-n(ē)-ī-ke   nõma   gīī.
   alligator lie-perf-infer-limit alligator become.thin

18 Ayæ̃ æ-bã-nõ kæ̃-kã-ta-wo ã-te,   ããka   nõma
   then how   do-3-pst-dubi say-ing exceedingly.long.time alligator

   õñõ-wē-te,   dagæ̃æ̃-ka   ēē-ke   be-wē-te   po
   lie-always-ing chonta.palm-fruit.id finish-limit drink-always-ing come

19 Æbãnõ kæ-da ã-te   põ.
   how   do-3d say-ing come

20 Kõwa.
   look

21 Ayæ̃ biwü a,   nõma   a.
   then bird see alligator see

22 Nõma   gīī.
   alligator become.thin

Giketa: The Alligator and the Bird

23 *Bi-tõ ni(y)æ ǣbã(ã)nõ ĩ-mi-'ĩ.*
   2-pn exclam.expl how be-2-emph

24 *Gẽã õŋõ-mõna-pa, kǣ-nã-maĩ.*
   together stand,stay-1d-asser eat-neg-like

25 *Biwü waa ĩ-ŋã.*
   bird good be-3

26 *Ĩ-ŋã nõma gū-bekāĩ*
   be-3 alligator become.thin

27 *Bi-tõ kǣ-te waa ĩ-mi-pa.*
   2-pn eat-ing good be-2-asser

28 *Bo-tõ kǣ-nã-maĩ ĩ-mõna-pa.*
   1-pn eat-neg-like be-1d-asser

29 *Mãnõ-maĩ kẽ-wẽ kǣ-mõna-ĩ ã-ñõ-mõna-te,*
   That-like live-always eat-1d-be say-when-1d-ing

   Kǣ-te kẽ-wẽ-kǣ-da-ĩ ã-mĩni-ta-wo, ã-mĩni-padi(y)æ.
   eat-ing live-always-incep-3d-be say-2p-pst-dubi say-2p-asser.exclam.expl

30 *Ayǣ nõma wodo wǣ-kæ kæ ba-kã.*
   Then alligator almost die-incep do become-3

31 *Kĩn(õ)ãte bi-tõ gūbe-dã-maĩ ĩ-mi-'i.*
   Why 2-pn get.thin-neg-like be-2-emph

32 *Bo-tõ õnõ-ke nãŋĩ gū be-te ba-bo.*
   1-pn just-limit lots get thin-ing become-1

33 *Kõwẽ mãnõ-maĩ ĩ-mo.*
   Always that-like be-1

34 *Ayǣ nõma wææte mõ ñõ, ayǣ awẽ-mõ kǣ diyǣ,*
   Then alligator in.turn sleep lie then secretly-perm.st eat exclam.expl

   a õŋõ.
   see stand

35 *Nõma, kĩn(õ)ãte, a-bo-te.*
   Alligator why see-1-ing

36 *Mõ-te-baĩ waa a.*
   sleep-ing-like good see

37 *A-yō-ŋā   biwii to   go-kā, ayæ̃ a-de   kæ̃.*
   See-when-3 bird   straight go-3   then see-mouth.id eat

38 *Eeeee babæ ā, bi-tō kæ̃-mi-pa.*
   Ah.ha! wild say 2-pn eat-2-asser

39 *Bi-tō babæ ā   ī-mi, bo-tō wa(a)-ē-mō   ī-mo.*
   2-pn wild say be-2   1-pn good-exist-perm.st be-pn

40 *Bo-tō ī-mo-te, kæ̃-nā-maī,   ā-mi, ōnō-ke   mæ̃   ō-ñō-mo*
   1-pn be-1-pn   eat-neg-like say-2 just-limit flat   lie-1

   gū̃ be-te   wæ̃-kæ̃   kæ̃, to go   awē-mō   kæ̃ diyæ̃.
   get thin-ing die-incep do   straight go secretly-perm.st eat exclam.expl

41 *Kōwē mānō-maī ī-mo.*
   Always that-like be-1

42 *Bo-tō ōnō-ke   doo   go-bo, kæ̃-mo.*
   1-pn just-limit long.since go-1   eat-1

43 *Mānō-maī ōnō-ke   ā-ta-bo-pa.*
   that-like just-limit say-pst-1-asser

44 *Nōma   nāŋī biwü ī-ŋā-te   pū-ŋā-ta-pa.*
   alligator lots bird be-3-ing mad-3-pst-asser

45 *Nōma   tōnō biwü, biwii-ke   nāŋī kæ̃-ŋā, nōma*
   alligator and bird bird-limit lots eat-3   alligator

   kæ̃-nā-maī   ōñō-n(ē)-ī-ke   kū be-kā-ta-pa.
   eat-not-like lie-perf-infer-limit get thin-3-pst-asser

46 *Ōnō-ŋadē taa-gade   ba-kā-ta-pa.*
   body-jaw.id hang.out-jaw.id became-3-pst-asser

47 *Manō-maī kæ̃-da-ta-pa.*
   that-like do-3d-pst-asser

48 *Mōni-tō biwü ī-ŋā-te, awī-nē-ŋā,   ā-mōni.*
   1p-pn   bird be-3-ing starve-perf-3 say-1p

49 *Nōma   ī-ŋā-te awī-nē-ŋā   gū̃ be-te   wodo   wæ̃-ŋā-ta-pa   ā-mōni.*
   alligator be-3-ing starve-perf-3 get thin-ing almost die-3-pst-asser say-1p

50 *Tōmāā mānō-maī ī-pa.*
   all   that-like be-asser

Free Translation 1. Long ago an alligator arrived and looked all around. He saw a little bird perched on a limb. 2. "Why do you live without eating?" he said to the bird. 3. "I always live like this. 4. I have a proposition to make you. 5. Let's have a contest, you down there on the ground and I up here on the limb. I won't eat and you don't eat anything either. Maybe we can fast for two years." 6. The alligator agreed. 7. "I won't eat anything either." 8. So they agreed. 9. After making the agreement, the alligator lay there and then went to sleep. 10. Whenever he woke up by night or day he looked up and saw the bird just perched on the limb, so he went to sleep again. 11. Every time the alligator woke up he looked up saying, "I wonder how the little bird is doing?" 12. There was the little bird way up there on the limb preening his feathers! 13. After the alligator lay there sleeping for a long long time, he wondered how the little bird was getting along and he looked up again. 14. There he was still preening his feathers! 15. "I, like you, am just sitting here," the little bird said. The alligator looked up. He lay there watching. There was the little bird just preening his feathers. 16. The alligator lay there for a very long time, and whenever he fell asleep the little bird would dart off the limb again and again, eat bugs and fly back to sit on the limb! 17. The alligator lay there getting thinner and thinner. 18, 19. Then the Waorani, realizing that the alligator had been lying there a very long time, were wondering how he was doing. But since a few chonta palm nuts had fallen, the Waorani said, "Let's go drink chonta drink." When they finished drinking, they returned wondering how the two were making out in their contest. 20. "Let's go see," they said. 21. There was the bird sitting there, and the alligator lying there. 22. As the alligator lay there he had become very thin. 23. "You there, how are you?" the Waorani asked. 24. "We're staying here together." 25. The little bird was fine. 26. But the alligator was very, very thin. 27. "You having eaten are fine," they said to the little bird. 28. "I say neither of us have eaten," he replied. 29. "When we both say that's the way we have been living you all say, 'So you say you two are living without eating, do you? We just don't believe you!'" 30. Then as time went by the alligator nearly died. 31. "How is it that you are not getting thin? 32. And I have become very, very thin?" he asked the little bird. 33. "I am always like this." 34. Then the alligator fell asleep again; and the little bird secretly flew off and ate, the little rascal, and quickly returned to sit on the limb! 35. But the alligator began to wonder what was going on. He decided to find out. 36. Pretending to be asleep, he peeped. 37. As he watched, the little bird darted off and gobbled up some bugs. 38. "Hey, you lied! You are eating! 39. You are a liar, I am the truthful one. 40. You told me and I lay there getting so thin I nearly died, and you secretly darted off and ate, you little rascal!" 41. "That's the way I always am. 42. I just quickly go and eat. 43. That's why I said what I did—just for fun!" 44. The alligator was furious at the little bird! 45. Between the alligator and the little bird, the bird alone ate lots; and because the alligator just lay there without eating, he got very thin. **46.** He was so thin his jaws became wrinkled! **47.** That's what happened to the two of them! **48.** So we call the little bird the ALLIGATOR STARVER. **49.** "He starved the alligator who got so thin he nearly died," we say. **50.** That's the end of the story.

Bluebird's Report

by Wiña

1 *Ænōmē-nãni apǽ-ne-kī-mo-?*
  lowland-3p   speak-mouth.id-fut-infer-1-?

2 *Ænōmē-nãni . . . mãnõ-maĩ . . .*
  lowland-3p   that-like

3 *Mōnõ ado-nãni apǽ-ne-kī-ĩ-mo-?*
  1p.excl one-3p   speak-mouth.id-fut-infer-1-?

4 *Kapitãã tōnõ tōmãã mao tōmãã tōmãã*
  pilot   with all   take all   all

  mao a-bo tōmãã-nãni mao a-ta   a   tōmãã-nãni nawǽ
  take see-1 all-3p   take see-pst see all-3p   look.up

  taa   gōŋǽ-nãni.
  go.out stand.up-3p

5 *Tōmãã-nãni ōkō-māka   taa   gōŋǽ-nãni a-ta-mōna-pa.*
  all-3p   house-roof.ridge.pole go.out stand.up-3p see-pst-1d-asser

6 *Toka-idi . . . Toka, Okata, tōmãã-nãni taa   gōŋǽ-nãni-ta-pa.*
  Toka-group Toka Okata all-3p   go.out stand.up-3p-pst-asser

7 *Tōmãã-nãni taa   gōŋǽ-nãni ōkiyǽ-nãni*
  all-3p   go.out stand.up-3p women-3p

  kaka   ẽ-mō-nãni-pōni,   ǽǽ-mǽ-no.
  achiote exist-face.id-3p-intens party-liquid.id-out.of

8 *Wa-dãni ayǽ weẽñǽ-ŋã mōŋǽ-nãni.*
  other-3p then child,baby-3 carry-3p

9 *Kaka   ẽ-mō-nãni   baki-dãni.*
  achiote exist-face.id-3p young.woman-3p

10 *Ayǽ weẽñǽ-nãni taa-te   a-dãni-ta-pa, ōkō-boyǽ.*
  then child-3p go.out-ing see-3p-pst-asser house-rounded.end

11 *Be-te   go gōŋǽ-te   a-dãni-pa.*
  drink-ing go stand.up-ing see-3p-asser

12, 13 *Kaka   ē-mō-nãni-pōni   gōŋǣ-nãni pikǣ-nãni.*
        achiote exist-face.id-3p-asser-intens stand.up-3p mature-3p

14 *Ayǣ wēēñǣ-nãni æ-bã(ã)-nō   a, awãã   nawæ*
    then child-3p   inter-all.id-twd.another see on.tree.trunk look.up

    gōŋǣ-te   a-dãni.
    stand.up-ing see-3p

15 *...go wai   wokǣ-ŋã a-yō-mo   Doka Doka Doka*
    ...go feet.up float-3   see-when-1   Doka Doka Doka

    kæ-te   kæ-d(ē)-ī-ke   wī   wǣ wæ-d(ē)-ī-ke....
    do-ing do-perf-infer-limit negative die cry-perf-infer-limit

16 *Pō-te   a-yō-mo   Doka*
    come-ing see-when-1 Doka

    wãtæ   wãtæ   wãŋǣ   wǣ   wæ-d(ē)-ī-ke   mōni-tō ã-mōni.
    long.time long.time become.weak die cry-perf-infer-limit 1p-pn   say-1p

17 *Bo-tõ pō-nō   pō-ŋã,   wǣ-te   nãñi   ñōŋǣ*
    1-pn   come-twd.another come-3   die-ing stretched.out lie.down

    pæopa-te   ñãni   ñōŋǣ   wæ-d(ē)-ī-ke.
    stiff-ing stretched.out lie.down   cry-perf-infer-limit

18 *Aka wǣpo   ã-te   wæ-d(ē)-ī-ke   mãmō   tō   pō-nō*
    Aka father say-ing cry-perf-infer-limit coming.toward straight pull-twd.another

    tō   pō-nō   ñã-ne-te   ñō   kæ kōmē   tanō   aa   wiyǣ-te ñō.
    straight pull-twd.another   wrap-ing   place do string first around wrap-ing lay

19 *Detæ, kōmē   tanō   aa   wiyǣ-ŋī-mi.*
    Detæ   string first around.and.around wrap-fut-2

20 *Ñaō   kæyǣ-te   ã-te   woyō-mo Nãka   tōnō Gǣmǣ tōnō.*
    loop tie.up-ing say-ing bury-1p Nãka   with Gǣmǣ   with

21 *Nǣkīmō mao   apǣ-ne-te   ēñē-te,   Nǣkīmō tapa   ōŋǣ*
    Nǣkīmō   come   speak-mouth-ing   hear-ing   Nǣkīmō spear grab

    mao   tǣnō   ã-te   wæǣ-i-dãni.
    carry spear say-ing down-com-2p

22 *Datæ ayǣ   iña-nãni   wǣpo...*
    Detæ   then dear.ones-3p father

23 *Detæ, tõ-mẽ-nani wǣpo, e owo-dãni a-te kæ-yõ*
   Detæ pn-?-3p   father wait lie.in.hammock-3p say-ing do-when

24 *Nãka owo-kã gi kõta-te apǣ-ne-dãni*
   Nãka lie.in.hammock-3 enter squat-ing speak-mouth.id-3p

   ẽñẽ-te a-te, wa wa wa wa ǣmǣ-nõ
   hear-ing see-ing other other other other other.side-twd.another

   gomõŋa ǣmǣ-nõ gomõŋa a-yõ
   beyond other.side-twd.another beyond see-when

25 *Iña-na kẽ-yǣ Nǣkīmõ õŋǣ mao tǣnõ-nõ-pa,*
   Dear.ones-2d fast-much Nǣkīmõ grab carry spear-twd.another-asser

   nãnogǣ wǣ-ŋǣī-pa ã-mi-ta-? a õŋõ-mi, ã-te
   wife die-surely-asser say-2-pst-? see stay-2 say-ing

   pū-ñõ-nãni Nãka, ã-ñõ-ŋã bi-tõ tǣnõ-kæ ã-mi põ-ta-mõ-pa.
   mad-when-3p Nãka say-when-3 2-pn spear-incep say-2 come-pst-1p.incl-asser

26 *Bi-tõ tǣnõ-kæ ã-mi-ta-wo-? Dikæ tǣnõ-mi-yaa.*
   2-pn spear-incep say-2-pst-dubi-? Never spear-2-emph.neg

27 *Nǣkīmõ ã-ŋã a-te Detæ gomõŋa gomõŋa kæ-kã.*
   Nǣkīmõ say-3 see-ing Detæ further further do-3

28 *Gomõŋa gomõŋa kæ-te wæ-d(ẽ)-ī-ke Aka aa wiyǣ.*
   further further do-ing cry-infer-infer-limit Aka around.and.around wrap

29 *Ã wæ-d(ẽ)-ī-ke ī-nõ ǣ-nõ-n(ẽ)-ī-ke*
   say cry-perf-infer-limit be-twd.another up-twd.another-perf-infer-limit

   wa wa wa-di(y)æ ayǣ kõmẽ w(æ)ǣ-nõ-mi
   another another another-expl.mild then string down-twd.another-2

   wææ̃ w(æ)-ǣ-nõ-mi nãmǣ ǣ-nõ.
   down down-twd.another-2 reflex up-twd.another

30 *Tõmãã aa wiyǣ aa wiyǣ aa wiyǣ-te*
   all over.and.over wrap over.and.over wrap over.and.over wrap-ing

   aa wiyǣ-te wææ̃-nõ ñaõ kæyǣ-ī.
   over.and.over wrap-ing down-twd.another crook tie-be

31 *Mãta ñaõ kæ-yǣi ã-te Aka ã, mãta ñaõ kæyǣ-ī ã-te*
   bring.out crook do-certain say-ing Aka say bring.out crook tie-be say-ing

æǣ-ŋã-te   taa-kã.
stand.up-3-ing go.out-3

32 *Ayǣ ǣnõwǣ-mǣ wǣ-te õñõ ñãni ñǣ-kæ-te ã-te   kæ-yõ-ŋã ayǣ*
   then lower-side die-ing lie flat tie-do-ing say-ing spear-when-3 then

   ãã gãnæ ǣ-ĩ-nẽ-mǣ-te wǣ-te õñõ ñãni ñǣ-kæ-te ã-te, æǣ-ŋã-te
   ???   ???   ???   die-ing lie flat tie-do-ing say-ing stand.up-3-ing

   taa-te   ĩña-nãni   tapa õŋǣ-te   mãta   yææ   tǣnõ-nãni.
   go.out-ing dear.one-3p spear grab-ing bring.out scream spear-ing

33 *Wodi wĩ-nõ.*
   take.off fled-twd.another

34 *Wĩ-nõ   wæ-d(ẽ)-ĩ-ke   giidãmǣ   tao   Ñai tõnõ*
   flee-twd.another cry-perf-infer-limit going.around.inside coming.out Ñai with

   Kǣmẽ wææ owo-da,   giidãmǣ   æ-de-kæ   tao
   Kǣmẽ   guard lie.in.hammock-? going.around.inside lift-mouth.id-incep go.out

   wĩ-nõ-kæ   kæ-yõ-te,   doobæ   ĩĩ-nãni põ-nãni wæ-d(ẽ)-ĩ-ke
   flee-twd.another do-when-ing already these-3p come-3p cry-perf-infer-limit

   æ-de-kæ   tao   go-kæ   kæ-te wæ-d(ẽ)-ĩ-ke   godãmǣ   ayǣ
   lift-mouth.id-incep go.out go-incep do-ing cry-perf-infer-limit going.around then

   godãmǣ   Kǣmẽ okagĩ yao   õñõ   mĩŋĩña wĩni wĩni kǣpo
   going.around Kǣmẽ   hair   reach.out stay suddenly wind wind do-hand.id

   (Expl Detæ ĩŋãte)   ĩ-na-nõ   tao   wĩ-nõ-nãni-pa   ã-te
   (Detæ, the object)   be-ind-twd.another go.out flee-twd.another-3p-asser say-ing

   Ñai pĩĩ-ñõ,   pæ   mã-te,   wĩni wĩni kæ-po-te,   dikagõ.
   Ñai mad-when arm.id hold-ing wind wind do-hand-ing dear.plug

   (Expl. to Detæ) ĩña-nãni   tao   go a-te,   tǣnõ-nãni-pa.
   ??? ??? ???   dear.one-3p go.out go see-ing spear-3p-asser

35 *Tǣnõ-nãni, e   a-b   kẽ-wẽ-ŋĩ   ã,*
   spear-3p   wait see-? live-always-fut say

   Detæ tõnõ ĩ-mõna-te   wati   tǣnõ-mĩni wæ-mõna.
   Detæ with be-1d-pn toss spear-2p   cry-1d

36 *W(æ)ǣ-mõ-e-dãni   ã-n(ẽ)-ĩ-ke   a   owo-da.*
   down-perm.st-?-3p   say-perf-infer-limit see lie.in.hammock-3p

37 *Ā-n(ē)-ī-ke*　　　*Ñai wati Detæ tōnō ī-mōna tænō-kæ*
　　say-perf-infer-limit　Ñai　toss　Detæ　with　be-1d　spear-incep

　　kæ-d(ē)-ī-ke　　*wati*　*tænō-mīni*　*wæ-mōna,*
　　do-perf-incep-limit　pierce　spear-2p　cry-1d

　　ā-n(ē)-ī-ke　　　*Ñai kaa*　*wæ.*
　　say-perf-infer-limit　Ñai boo.hoo cry

38 *Wæ-d(ē)-ī-ke*　　*Detæ*　*kæ*　*tayǽpo*　*tayǽpo*　*kæ-dāni. Wekātoke, mao*
　　cry-perf-infer-limit　Detæ　spear　many　　many　spear-3p　Wekātoke　come

　　yao ōŋō-ŋā Wekātoke tao　nǽæ-po-bo　　　wī-nō-ŋī　　　　　ā-te
　　grab stay-3　Wekatoke　go.out restrain-hand.id-1 flee-twd.another-fut say-ing

　　kæ-kā,　ōnōke mānō-maī ā-ŋā　a-te　Detæ wodi　　ao　ā-te.
　　do-3　just　that-like　say-3 see-ing Detæ disappear O.K. say-ing

39 *Nǽnæ　ǽmǽ-kapo　ōnōke yao　ōŋō-ŋā*
　　Nǽnæ　other.side-knee.id just　reach.out stay-3

40 *Yǽæ　wæ-d(ē)-ī-ke　tapa togo-kæ　togo-kæ　kæ wæ-d(ē)-ī-ke.*
　　scream cry-perf-infer-limit spear poke-incep poke-incep do cry-perf-infer-limit

41 *Ayǽ kæ-te　　ī-maī　bo-tō　ñānō-ī　owo-bo,　　　　ode-mō*
　　then spear-ing be-like 1-pn fastened-be stay.in.hammock-1 hole-perm.st

　　ī-maī owo-bo
　　be-like stay.in.hammock-1

42 *Ī-maī ñānō-ī　　owo-da　　　　yǽæ　wæ yǽæ　wæ.*
　　be-like fastened-be stay.in.hammock-3d scream cry scream cry

43 *Ōkaye iñōmō　owo　　　　ī-te, wæ wāānā*
　　Ōkaye right.here stay.in.hammock be-ing cry her.mother

　　wodi,　Wēmōka wodi,　wæ,　Nǽkīmō iyigīī　ī-maī
　　departed Wēmōka departed die Nǽkīmō close.by be-like

　　owo-d(ē)-ī-ke　　　　māŋī　　　bæi ōŋō (Detæ ī-ŋā-te).
　　stay.in.hammock-perf-infer-limit come.toward held stay (Detæ be-3-ing)

44 *Ayǽ Nǽkīmō māŋī　　yao　ōŋō-te boo tænō-ŋā tao*
　　then Nǽkīmō come.toward reach.out stay-ing pierce spear-3 go.out

　　tǽ　wæǽ.
　　plunk down

45 *Ayǽ Nǽkīmō tǽnō-ŋã godomēke tao   go-w(ǽ)ǽ-te*
   then Nǽkīmō spear-3   further.on go.out (go-down).fall-ing

   wǽǽ   ūūū   wæ-d(ē)-ī-ke   doobæ wǽ.
   fell.down (groan) cry-perf-infer-limit already die

46 *Wati wati tǽnō-nãni wæ-d(ē)-ī-ke.*
   toss toss spear-3p cry-perf-infer-limit

47 *Mãni-nō   tǽnō-nãni wæ-d(ē)-ī-ke   wããnã   wodi   wǽ*
   that-twd.another spear-3p cry-perf-infer-limit her.mother departed die

   wæ-d(ē)-ī-ke,   Õmækoo wǽ a-wæ-dō   ã-te
   cry-perf-infer-limit Õmækoo die know-cry-twd.another say-ing

   wæ-d(ē)-ī-ke.
   cry-perf-infer-limit

48 *Aka, Detæ ī-te   e   a-mini daa wěmō-i-dãni ã-te   wæ-yō-ŋã-te*
   Aka Detæ be-ing wait see-2p push bury-3p-com-2p say-ing cry-when-3-ing

   Aka ūñã-nãni   wiaa ǽǽ-te   kōwě go-dãni wæ-d(ē)-ī-ke
   Aka dear.one-3p pull take-ing always go-3p cry-perf-infer-limit

   ōkō-boyǽ   a-de-kæ   wiaa ã-te   go-dãni wæ-d(ē)-ī-ke
   house-rounded.end see-mouth-incep pull say-ing go-3p cry-perf-infer-limit

   tōmããã-nãni.
   all-3p

49 *Kǽmě, gīñě gīñě tǽnō-nãni a-wæ-dō   kowodě němǽ*
   Kǽmě afraid afraid spear-3p know-cry-twd.another outsiders stay.with

   go-mō   ōō   wǽ-mō.
   go-1p.inc shoot die-1p.excl

50 *Ã-ně   kō-mōni a-de-kæ.*
   say-had squat-1p see-mouth.id-incep

Comment: From this point on the report is being reported by another person who listened to the tape and reported what Wiña had said. Notice a repeat of part of sentence 49 with second person reporting.

49, 50 ... *Kowodě němǽ go-mō ōō   wǽ-mō ã ayǽ*
              outsiders stay.with go-1p.inc shoot die-1p.inc say then

ã-nẽ kõ-mõni akii.
say-had squat-1p here

51 *Kæ̃to iñõmõ mãnõ pe iñã-nãni æi-dãni-ta-pa.*
 Kæ̃to here come.toward call dear.one-3p go.upriver-3p-pst-asser

52 *Æb(ã)ãnõ kæ-kĩ ã-ŋã Okæ̃mæ̃ kü-te õŋõ-te wæ-d(ẽ)-ĩ-ke*
 What do-fut say-3 Okæ̃mæ̃ enter-ing stay-ing cry-perf-infer-limit

 wãã̃nã wodi Õmækoo wæ̃-ŋã a-wæ-dõ
 her.mother departed Õmækoo die-3 know-cry-twd.another

 ã-te, wæ, ayæ̃ ã-nẽ eyekü ĩ-pa, wa-kõ-nẽ
 say-ing cry then say-perf close.by be-asser other-house.id-in

Free Translation 1. Shall I speak of the Downriver Waorani? 2. The Downriver group—this is the way it was . . . 3. We (excl) . . . Shall I speak of our own group? 4. I went with the Captain (pilot) and he took me (in the plane) so I could see it all—I saw everything. All of them looked up. Going outside the house they stood there and we saw them. 5. All of them, going outside the house stood on the roof beam of the house and we saw them. (Explanation: Kadæ, deceased Owæ̃'s child, and Wanẽ were on the roof.) 6. There was Toka's family group, Toka, Okata, all of them went outside and stood there. 7. All of them, the women with achiote (red coloring) on their faces, they were having a drinking party. 8. There were others, some of them were carrying their babies in dark-cloth slings. 9. The unmarried girls had their faces painted with achiote. 10. Then I saw the children come out to the yard just outside the rounded-end of the house. 11. They were drinking (at the party), but they went and stood there when they saw us. 12, 13. The older ones were standing there too. They had their faces painted very red with achiote. 14. Then the children, how did we see them, they were all standing on a tree trunk looking up and watching the plane.

[Same report but later on the tape:] 15. I went and was there in a hammock when I saw Doka who had been speared. Having been speared, he didn't die. It was horrible. [Explanation: he could no longer stand up, it was frightening.] 16. Having come, as I watched, we said, "It has been a long time. Doka is very weak and dying. How very sad to see it." 17. As I went toward him, she came. Dying he was stretched out and lying there being stiff [explanation: from being tied up not from being dead], he was stretched out and lying there. It was awful. 18. Crying, "My father!" Aka wound him around and around, pulling the string tight. First wrapping him around and around with string, she laid him there. 19. "Detæ, you wrap him up first." [Explanation: they tied the victim alive in his hammock, winding it around with string because he will rot.] 20. "Tie him up and let Nanka, Gǣmǣ, and me bury him."

21. When they went and told Nǣkĭmõ what had happened, Nǣkĭmõ grabbed his spear with the intention of spearing to avenge the death (of his relative) and said, "Let's go down there." 22. Detæ then said, "Dear ones, father...." 23. When Detæ saw that they just stayed in their hammocks without doing anything about it, she said (to herself), "It is their father (who has been speared)!" 24. Nãka was swinging in his hammock when others entered and squatting down talked about it. He realized that many others even from a distance knew. 25. Someone said, "You two fellows, hurry up! Nǣkĭmõ has already grabbed his spear and gone off to kill. 'His wife will surely die,' did you not say? What are you doing staying here?" And they were furious as they said it. "When Nãka said, 'You should spear,' that's why we came." 26. "Did you say I told you to spear? I never said you should spear! I never said any such thing!" 27. After Nǣkĭmõ said that, Detæ spread the news further and further. 28. As she did that just causing more trouble, Aka was wrapping the string around and around. 29. As that was being said, as sad as it made her, she continued to take the string up and over, up and over. Then, "What about another?" she asked. She did it another time. Then she said, "You take it around and down the other side, and I myself will pull it up." 30. They covered the whole body. Over and over they wrapped it, over and over wrapping and wrapping it, then down on the other side, then it was tied. 31. "Take it out. Make a knot loop. It must be tied," Aka said. So they take it out in the clearing, they make a knot loop and it was tied in a knot. Saying this, she stood up and went outside. 32. Then upside down dying he lay [Owæ, Detæ's husband] tied and flat, they said, when he speared, ? saying he lay there dying, flat and tied up, and as she was standing up to go out, the fellows grabbed their spears and taking them out, yelling they speared her. 33. They escaped and fled! 34. After they fled—it was so terrible! They went around inside the house and came out on the other side. Ñai and Kǣmẽ were swinging in their hammocks watching (guarding). When they were going around inside (the house) to lift up the thatch to flee, immediately these others arrived. How scared we were! As they were lifting the thatch in order to escape, going around and going around someone grabbed and held [Detæ] suddenly and winding it around her hand, Detæ said, "They must be fleeing in that direction out of the house." Ñai when she was mad about it, grabbed [Detæ] and wrapping [Detæ's] hair around her hand, she pulled out [Detæ's] ear plugs. Seeing the dear ones about to escape, they speared them. 35. As they speared, we said, "Watch what you are doing! Let us live. We don't want you to thrust us through with your spears—Detæ and the two of us. 36. Let us die," they said, and the two of them just stayed in their hammocks. 37. After they said

that, Ñai when they were about to spear Detæ and me, both of us, said "You all are going to throw your spears at us and both of us are terrified." And when she said that, Ñai began to cry. **38.** They speared Detæ many many times, and Wikãtoke coming grabbed and held her. "Wikãtoke run away, I will hold her, flee!" [And when he said that he did so: Detæ, who is now dead, agreed with him.] **39.** Nǽnæ grabbed the other knee. **40.** Because she screamed, the spear was poked at her again and again, and she was petrified! **41.** Then after they did that, like this I was swinging in my hammock which was hung right near the door, like this I swung in my hammock. **42.** And the other two were swinging in their hammocks like this, yelling and screaming. **43.** Onkaye who was swinging in her hammock right there cried for her departed mother, for Wěmõka who was dead. Nǽkĭmõ, since he was in his hammock, close by like this, hurried toward Detæ and grabbed and held her. **44.** Then Nǽkĭmõ coming forward, grabbed and held her and pierced her with his spear and she stumbled out and fell down. **45.** Then Nǽkĭmõ speared (again) and further on she fell down. "Uh uh uh," she groaned. It was pathetic! And she died! **46.** They tossed their spears (at her) again and again. What a fearsome sight! **47.** Like that they speared. It was repulsive. Their mother, now departed, died. It was an awful mess! "I fear Omækoo is dead," saying he was sad. **48.** Aka (said), "Let Detæ alone and let us bury the dead," she insisted while she was crying. Aka said, "Dear ones, please pull and take him to bury. Have mercy on me!" But they, all of them, were pulling an escape hole in the thatch, and left without helping her at all! **49.** "Kǽmě I'm terribly afraid! I know they are going to spear us! Let's us (incl) go to stay with the outsiders, and if they shoot us we'll just die!" **50.** And when she had said that, someone said, "Let's squat down here."

[From this point on the report is being reported by another person who listened to the tape and reported what Wiña had said. Notice a repeat of sentences 49 and 50 with second person reporting.]

49 "Let's us (inclusive) go to stay with the outsiders, if they shoot us we will just die," she said. **50.** Then, when she had said that, someone said, "Let's squat down here." **51.** When Kǽnto came and called, the dear ones (in group) went on upriver. **52.** "What will you do," he said, "Okæmæ has come to the house and is staying. His mother now departed [or as good as dead] has died, I fear." And she cried. Then, after she had said that, "Here, close by in the other house . . ."

Waorani Earholes

by Akawo

1. *Mānō-maī godō-mōka-te a-de(ē)-ī-ke,   māniñōmō bi-tō a-bi-?*
   that-like   pull-ear.id-ing   see-perf-infer-limit   right.here   2-pn see-2-?

   māni eye-gō-ŋa   mānō-maī ōpite māniñōmō kæ-d(ē)-ī-ke
   this   near-finger.id-place   that-like   hole   right.here   do-perf-infer-limit

   māniñōmō yædæ tai ī-ŋō-ŋa   māniñōmō-nō   wa
   right.here   extend out ve-finger.id-place   right.here.at.this.place   another

   tii tǣnō-mōka-dāni-pa.
   jab spear-ear.id-3p-asser

2. *Tǣnō-mōka-d(e)-ī-ke ñīī-po   kæ-d(e)-ī-ke   ǣmǣ-mōka-gō*
   spear-ear-perf-infer-limit let.go-hand do-perf-infer-limit other.side-ear-finger

   ado-baī yædæ godō yædæ godō kæ-d(ē)-ī-ke   māniñōmō wa
   one-like extend pull extend pull do-perf-infer-limit right.here   another

   tii tǣnō-mōka-dāni-pa.
   jab spear-ear-3p-asser

3. *Oto-mē-ŋa   tii, ba,   māni edæ   māni tǣnō-mōka-ī.*
   certain.plant-vine-with jab just.look! this   expl.mild this   spear-ear-be

4. *Māni tǣnō-mōka īmō   māni ad(o)-ōnæ-ke ī-pa.*
   this   spear-ear.id next.day this   one-day.id-limit be-asser

5. *Māni-ŋō-ŋa   koyiwǣ ē-ā   koye-gō   ē-nē-te*
   this-finger-place acid.plant exist-say certain.plant-finger/stick exist-insides-ing

   māmō ootogǣ-te wido   kæ-d(ē)-ī-ke   mī-nē tii-mōka-dāni.
   bring   pull.out-ing throw.out do-perf-infer-limit put-in fit-ear-3p

6. *Ēka-yǣ   a-te   mānō-maī ē-nē-mō   a-kī-mi.*
   later-much see-ing that-like   exist-insides.id-perm.st see-fut-2

7. *Ōō, mānō-maī tǣnō-mōka-kā wæ-wē-te   ye-gō   ba-mōka-te.*
   ouch that-like   spear-ear-3   cry-always-ing big-stick become-ear-ing

8. *Gāmǣ-mōka-te kē-wē-mo   wepǣ māniñōmō tkhu tkhu wæǣ,*
   heal-ear.id-ing   live-always-1 blood right.here   spurt spurt down

mãniñõmõ wææ̃-ŋã.
right.here down-3

9   *Mãniñõmõ pæ̃-kæ pæ̃-kæ̃ pæ̃-kæ̃ mãnõ-maĩ æ̃mæ̃-mõka*
    right.here swell-incep swell-incep swell-incep that-like other.side-ear.id

    pæ̃-kæ̃ pæ̃-kæ̃ pæ̃-kæ̃ mãnõ-maĩ.
    swell-incep swell-incep swell-incep that-like

10 *Ñõõ   bigitĩ-n(ẽ)-ĩ-ke   æ   kæ ĩ-kæ-tá-(-pa).*
    hammock caught.in.holes-perf-infer-limit sharp hurt be-incep-pst-(asser)

11 *Ñõõ   bigitĩ-n(e)-ĩ-ke   æ   kæ ĩ-kæ-tá(-pa).*
    hammock caught.in.holes-perf-infer-limit sharp hurt be-incep-pst-asser

12 *Ĩñõmõ ĩñõmõ õnõke kæ-dãmaĩ wa   tii æ̃mæ̃-nõ   wa*
    there there just do-neg   another jab other.side-twd.another another

    tii mãnõ-kado-te,   õnõmõka tãno õnõkado güdēmē ye-kẽ-nẽ
    jab make.hole-nose.id-ing ear   first nose   very.small large-must-perf

    ñõwo-ke pikæ̃-mo ba-te   wa   tii æ̃mæ̃-kado wa   tii,
    now-limit mature-1 become-ing   another jab other.side-nose another jab

    (Tamata-baĩ mãnõ-kado-dãni-pa.)   pæ̃-kæ   pæ̃-kæ   mẽ-ñõ
    (Tamata-like make.hole-nose-3p-asser) swell-incep swell-incep get.large-when

    ado-gõ-ke   daa tĩ-kado-te.
    one-finger-stick-limit push fit.in.hole-nose-ing

13 *(Mãnõ-kado-dã-maĩ)   ĩ-te   a-te   ayæmõ (kowæ̃) obe õñõ-pa*
    make.hole-nose-neg-like be-ing see-ing bird   (turkey) boa lie-asser

    ã-nãni-pa.
    say-3p-asser

14 *Wẽ(ẽ)ñæ̃-ŋã Iniwa gõpo-te   wæ-pa.*
    child-3   Iniwa being.selfish-ing cry-asser

15 *Wẽ(ẽ)ñæ̃-ŋã gõpo-te   wæ-pa.*
    child-3   being.selfish-ing cry-asser

16 *Baĩ tõnõ   a-te   (tewæ̃   ĩ-te,) Ta-i-da   ã-mo.*
    Baĩ and/with see-ing chonta.palm be-ing come.out-com-2d say-1

17 *Mãnõ-maĩ mæ̃mæ̃   mãnõ-mõka-kã*
    that-like grandfather make.hole-ear.id-3

18 *Dikagõ.*
    ear.plugs

19 *Bo-tõ wǽmǽ   Nẽmõka peto-gõ   wao wao wĩna-te   bo-tõ*
    1-pn   grandfather Nẽmõka peto.palm-stick shave shave whittle-ing 1-pn

    wepǽ kæ-bo ĩ-n(e)-ĩ-ke   ææ ææ ũ-ŋã õmõmoke-dõ
    blood do-1   be-perf-infer-limit so so this-3 my.grandchild-twd.another

    wepǽ kæ-d(e)-ĩ-ke   ba-mõka   kẽwẽ. Ææ ñõwo ĩkæ   Ñǽno
    blood do-perf-infer-limit   whole-ear.id live so now   be-incep Ñǽno

    ĩ-ŋã ã-nãni   ẽñẽ-mo-mǽ   ã-ŋẽ-nẽ.
    be-3 say-3p   hear-1-deris   say-admon-perf

20 *Baki-da   ba-d(ẽ)-ĩ-ke   wẽẽñǽ-ŋã awẽmõ   to-te*
    female.unmarried-3h become-perf-infer-limit   child-3   secretly laugh-ing

    ẽ-nẽ-te.
    exist-insides.id-ing

21 *Wabãnõ woo   woo   yædẽmadã wẽmaĩ-ŋã, kæ-mõka-te   a-te*
    Perhaps throb throb pregnant dark-be-3 hurt-ear.id-ing see-ing

    wide   põnẽ   ĩ-pa,   dikagõ   kæ-mõka-te   wide
    thoroughly remember is-asser ear.plug hurt-ear.id-ing thoroughly

    põnẽ   ĩ-pa.
    remember is-asser

22 *Nãno-gǽ-nãni   õŋõ-kapo-te   a-te   to-ĩ   ĩ-pa,   doo-dãni*
    their-spouse-3p   sit/stay-knee.id-ing see-ing laugh-be be-asser long.ago-3p

    ã-nõ-nãni-pa.
    say.cont.pst-3p-asser

23 *Ææ mãnõ-maĩ   ã-nãni mõni-tõ doo-põni   ĩ-ñõ-mõ*
    so that-like say-3p 1p-pn   long.ago-intens here

    ea-dõ-mõni-pa.
    desist-cont.pst-1p-asser

24 *Mǽmǽ   Nẽmõka ã-ŋã   wæ-yõ-mo   peto-gõ   mǽ-te   ǽǽ-ŋĩ-ŋã.*
    grandfather Nẽmõka say-3 cry-when-1 certain.palm-stick break-ing take-fut-3

25 *Mǽ-te   wao   wao   wĩna-te,   ǽǽ-ŋã Waawǽ (bipĩke   ã-mi)*
    break-ing shave shave whittle-ing take-3 Waawǽ grandfather's.brother say-2

botōmokā   ta-kā-i   mānō-mōka-bo-e.
my.grandchild go.out-3-com make.hole-ear.id-1-permis

26 Ā wæ-d(ē)-ī-ke   ao ā-te   taa   tǣ   kōta-bo.
   say cry-perf-infer-limit OK say-ing come.out plunk sit.squat-1

27 Ñōnǣ godō ñōnǣ godō ñōnǣ godō ñōnǣ godō kæ-mōka-kā
   bamboo pull bamboo pull bamboo pull bamboo pull hurt-ear.id-3

   wæ-yō-mo   ǣmǣ-mōka-tai   mānō-maī ñōnǣ ñōnǣ ñōnǣ
   cry-when-1 other.side-ear.id-flesh.id that-like bamboo bamboo bamboo

   go-po-d(ē)-ī-ke   dikagō.
   push-finger/hand.id-perf-infer-limit ear.plug

28 Mānō-maī kæ-d(ē)-ī-ke   nānō   peto-gō   doo-gǣ-ŋa-te
   that-like hurt-perf-infer-limit that.one certain.palm-long/thin long-?-?-ing

   æǣ-nē-ŋō-ka, ū   ba-tai   ī-ñō-mō   w(æ)ǣ-nō
   take-perf-stick-with here whole-flesh.id be-where-perm.st down-twd.another

   gao   pō-i,   mānō-maī gō-nō-te   mānō-mōka-dāni-pa.
   close come-com that-like set-twd.another-ing make.hole-ear.id-3p-asser

29 Ōnōke e   ōŋō.
   just desist stay

30 Mānō-mai mānō-maī godo-mōka-te mānō-maī godo-mōka-te waa
   that-like that-like pull-ear.id-ing that-like pull-ear.id-ing well

   a-d(ē)-ī-ke   māniñōmō mānō-mōka-dāni-pa.
   see-perf-infer-limit there   make.hole-ear.id-3p-asser

31 E w(æ)ǣ-nō   e   ōŋō e   iñǣ æǣ-mōka   mānō-maī
   desist down-twd.another desist stay desist turn take-ear.id that-like

   ī-ŋā-te a-yǣ.
   be-3-ing see-much

32 Awa wodi   ye-kē-nē   doo   kæ-ī-ŋā.
   Awo departed bigger-admon-perf long.since do-be-3

33 Gaakamō-(ŋ)aa yi-kē-nē   ñōwo nāno ī(ī)-ñidē   mānō-maī
   gaakamō-calling big-admon-perf now that.one this-at.this.time that-like

   mānī-ŋō   (boye-ŋō)   daa,   mānī-ŋō   daa
   this-finger.id;long/thin boye.plant-stick push.through this-finger.id push.through

mănĭ-ŋŏ̆ daa, mănĭ-po.
this-stick push.through this-hand.id

34 *Awæ̆payegŏ̆ æmæ̆wo wătæ di-pa (we-pæ̆ ta-dă-maĭ*
thumb for.the.last.time little.while stop-asser (blood go.out-neg-like

dæ ă-pa) wătæ di-yŏ̄ gamæ̆-ñŏ̆ w(æ)æ̆-ñŏ̆
none say-asser) little.while stop-when heals.over-when down-when

(ñæ̆næ̆-ŋadē owo yæ̆æ̆-te w(æ)æ̆-nŏ̆) ŏ̄-to gamē-to mæ̆
big-very lie.in.hammock ?-ing down-twd.another ?-stick balsa-stick flat

daa tĭĭ-mŏ̄ka dikamŏ̄ daa tĭĭ-mŏ̄ka-te
push.through fit.in.hole-ear.id ear.plug push.through fit.in.hole-ear.id-ing

daa tĭĭ-mŏ̄ka-te ñŏ̄næ̆ ñŏ̄næ̆ ñŏ̄næ̆ wæ̆æ̆-pa
push.through fit.in.hole-ear.id-ing bamboo bamboo bamboo down-asser

ñæ̆næ̆-ŋadē ba-ĭ-kæ-ta-pa.
big-very become-be-incep-pst-asser

35 *Mănŏ̄-maĭ kæ-te Awo wodē doo kæ-dē-ŋă̆.*
that-like do-ing Awo departed already do-perf-3

36 *Ñæ̆næ̆-ŋadē ba a-te bi-tŏ̆ ĭ-mi-te ă-te. a-te mănŏ̄-maĭ*
big-very become see-ing 2-pn be-2-ing say-ing see-ing that-like

ă-pa, ēñē-kæ-b(i)-ĭ-pa ă-te.
say-asser obey-incep-2-infer-asser say-ing

37 *Ñŏ̄wo ĭ-te năno æ̆æ̆-te go-baĭ, ĭ-po-ga*
recently be-ing that-one take-ing go-like be-hand.id-together

ado-po-ga ĭ-nŏ̆-pa, mănĭ-po-ga ĭ-ŋă̆.
one-hand-together be-cont.pst-asser that-hand.id-together is-3

38 *Ado-baĭ batadæ (ba-yŏ̆-te) doobæ kæ-dē-ŋă̆ ĭ-ŋă̆-pa.*
one-like puberty (become-when-ing) already do-perf-3 be-3-asser

39 *Pŏ̄nē-mĭni mănŏ̄-mŏ̄ka kæ-bo-ĭ-pa.*
remember-2p make.hole.in-ear.id do-1-infer-asser

Năpai-da mĭna wēē-ŋă̆ ba-mŏ̄ka-kă̆ ĭ-ŋă̆-pa.
Năpai-2h 2h child-3 whole-ear.id-3 is-3-asser

40 *Æ̆æ̆-te pŏ̄nŏ̆-mĭna bo-tŏ̆ momokă̆ mănŏ̄-mŏ̄ka-bo-e-da,*
take-ing bring-2h 1-pn grandchild make.hole-ear.id-1-permis-2h

(Nēmōka ã)   ã-n(ē)-ī-ke   Awo wodi   ī-ŋā-te ǣmǣ-mōka
(Nēmōka   says) say-perf-infer-limit Awo departed be-3-ing other.side-ear.id

poda-ī   ǣmǣ-mōka poda-ī   mānō-maī mānō-mōka-tǣ.
push.through-be other.ear.id push.through-be that-like that-ear.id-?

dikagō   poda   poda   mānō-mōkatē̃.
ear.plug push.through   push.through make.hole-ear.id-ing

41 Mānō-mōka-te   ado-baī   daa   daa   daa   tīūmōka   ye-gō
   make.hole-ear.id-ing one-like push push push fit.in-ear.id big-finger-stick

ē-mōka-ī kǣ-dō-nā-pa. (Awo)
exist-ear.id-be do-cont.pst-3h-asser (Awo)

Free Translation 1. When they pull the ear like this—right here do you see this? Here where my finger is? When they make a hole right here, right here where I am pulling out the lobe of the ear, that is the place where they jab and pierce the ear. 2. After they have pierced that ear, then they let it go. Then in the same way they pull out and pull down the ear on the other side, and they jab and pierce the other ear right there. 3. Then they force into the hole the otomẽ-vine. Just push it in. Wow! It hurt! [explanation: because the vine is an acid-like vine and burns!] Right there where it was pierced. 4. Right here it is pierced. The next day is the first day (of the process). 5. Then on the third day (literally, "on this finger"—counting from the little finger to the middle finger and touching it with the thumb) there is a certain tree, the coyi tree, and they bring the inside of the stem of that tree, and they pull out the former substance and throw it away, then they stuff the hole with this new fiber. 6. Later on we will show you that fiber from the inside of the stem. 7. Ouch! The one who has the pierced ear really has a bad time, especially when the hole is filled with a big stick. 8. (When they did it to me) my ear healed over . . . . The blood spurted out and ran down. 9. Then right there it swelled and swelled and swelled and like that, right here on the other ear it swelled and swelled and swelled. 10. And when I got caught in the holes of my hammock it would really cause a sharp hurt. 11. Yes it really hurt very much if one would get it caught in the holes of the hammock! 12. (Next) here and here (pointing to the septum of the nose) if it has never been done they pierce one side and then the other side, making tiny holes in the nose. They pierce the ears first, and then the very small holes (of the ear) must become big. More recently when I became mature, one side of my nose was pierced and then the other side. (They pierce the nose when one is like Tamata in age—16 years or so.) The nose swells and swells, and when it is swollen a thorn is pushed through the hole. 13. "When no noseholes are made, the boa lies (on the trail)," they say. [Explanation: the boa will block your way to Heaven when you die.] **14.** When he was a child, Iniwa was crying because they were selfish (with meat, the jungle turkey which they had brought.) **15.** When he was just a child he was crying when they were selfish (with their jungle turkey meat). **16, 17.** Along with Bai, "Come out you two," Grandfather called to them, and he had a tewæ palm (thorn) in his hand and made earholes in their ears.

18. Now I will tell you about ear plugs. **19.** My grandfather Nemonka was whittling long thin peto palm sticks when I menstruated for the first time. He said, "So, this is one who is my own granddaughter. She has begun to menstruate and she hasn't had her ears pierced, (so now I am going to do it.)" It was Ñæno to whom they said, "You should have obeyed! You know better than to act like that! [explanation: Ñæno had run off with another girl's husband.] **20, 21.** When you become a potential mother perhaps when your ears hurt very much you will remember if you first become pregnant with an illegitimate child. When the pregnancy reaches the point of making the dark navel line, you will throb with labor pains worse than the throbbing in your ears. That's what the ear plugs are for (to keep you from such action). **22.** If they are married, staying on their knees is flirting, the great-grandparents told me. **23.** So, when they talked like that, when we were young long ago where we lived, we did not act in that way. **24.** I cried when grandfather Nemonka said he would go out and break off a long thin piece of peto palm. **25.** Having broken it off, as he was whittling it down to a slim piece, when he got it, Waawæ, you call him GRANDFATHER'S BROTHER said to me, "Granddaughter, go outside, and let me make holes in your ears." **26.** When he said that I groaned inwardly, but had to agree so I went outside and squatted down. **27.** The bamboo (sliver) was pulled through time and again and the ear hurt. When I cried, changing to the other ear lobe he pulled the bamboo through by hand again and again (for the) earplug. **28.** When they had done that, that one with the long thin peto palm dart which he had gone out to get, here where the ear is only flesh (the lobe) right there, he said, "Bend over! Come closer!" Like that, standing there, they made holes in my earlobes. **29.** "Now just wait." **30.** Like that pulling the ear again and again then looking at it carefully, right here they made holes in my ears. **31.** "Be careful! Stoop over! Stay there! Be careful! Turn the other ear!" Like that . . . still they worked on it. **32.** Awo, who's now dead, thought "It must be bigger, it was done long ago." [Explanation: she was referring to an ear perforation in process.] **33.** "Gaakamõ(ŋ)..a," she called to Gaakamõ. Then she thought, "It must be bigger, Gaakamõ's earholes must be bigger by this time. Now this long thin br̥ye thorn must be pushed into the hole, again and again, this many times. Then on the fifth day it will be all dried up. **34.** On the fifth day they do it for the last time. Then when it dries up, when it heals over, a big stick of balsa wood is pulled down [Explanation: from the overhead swinging basket hung over the fire]. Then an earplug is cut off the big piece and stuffed into the hole in the ear again and again. And the same is done with a big stone. The earholes used to get very big. **35.** Doing it like that Awo, who is now dead, finished the process. **36.** When it has become big, seeing that it has, they say to you, "Now you are going to hear/obey" [Explanation: and not live loosely]. **37.** Now, just recently it was an unmarried girl someone must have taken off. It was eleven days ago. It is now that many days. **38.** It should have been done [ears should have been perforated] for anyone that age [who has reached puberty]. **39.** [Nẽmõka said to me,] "Let me perforate your ears so you will remember. Nampai, your daughter has no earholes. **40.** Bring her to me. She is my grandchild, and you let me make holes in her ears." Then he said to Awo, who is now dead, "Push it through one ear and then the other and having made earholes like that they pushed an earplug through one side and then the other, to make the holes big enough." **41.** Then having pierced the ear she ran a thorn through the hole again and again, a big long one, and what she did is still there in the ear.

www.ingramcontent.com/pod-product-compliance
Lightning Source LLC
Chambersburg PA
CBHW051811230426
43672CB00012B/2699